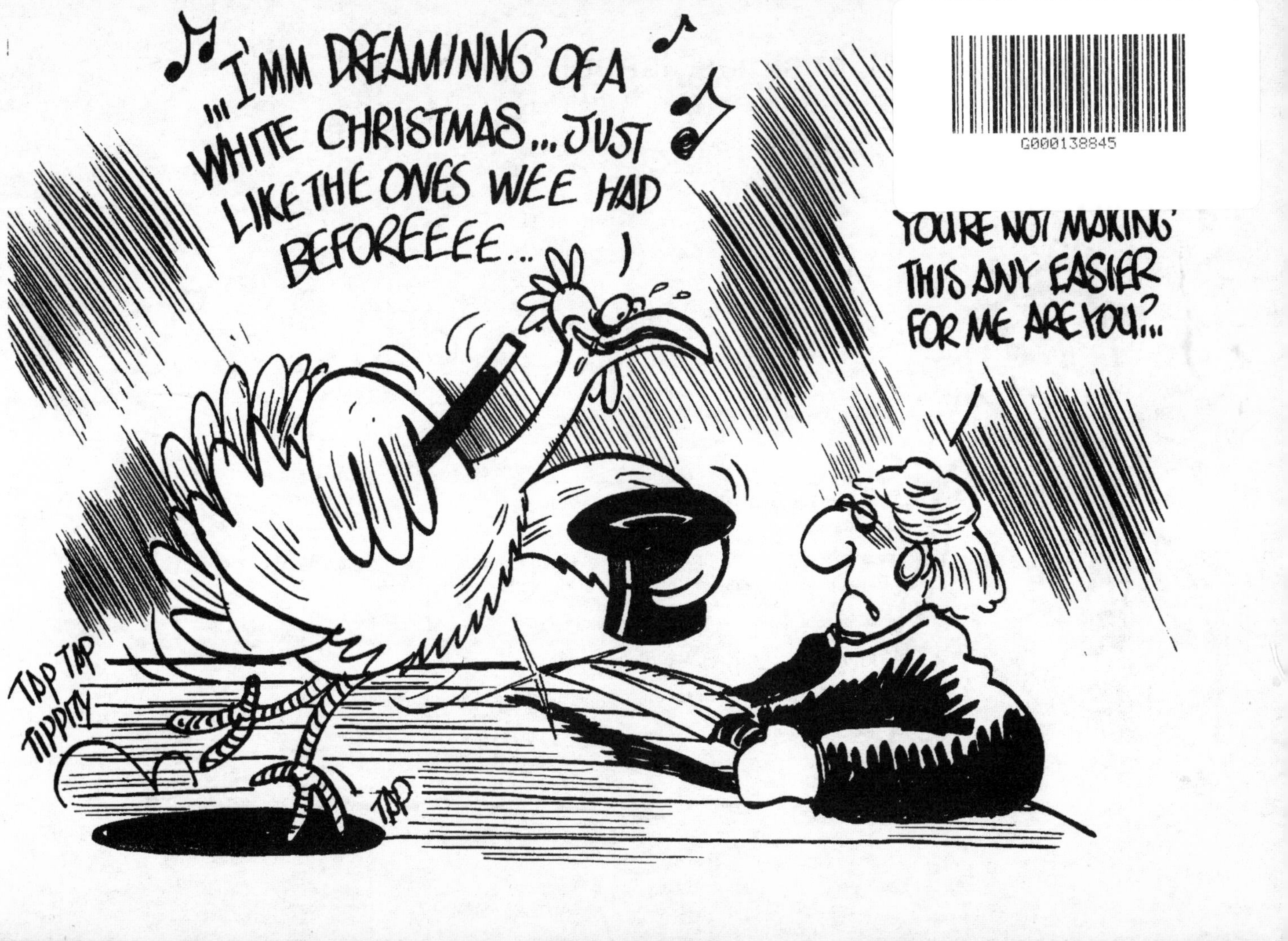
...I'MM DREAMINNG OF A WHITE CHRISTMAS... JUST LIKE THE ONES WEE HAD BEFOREEEEE...
YOU'RE NOT MAKING THIS ANY EASIER FOR ME ARE YOU?...
TAP TAP TIPPITY
TAP

Happy Christmas, Isabel

First published in 1997 by
The Blackstaff Press Limited
3 Galway Park, Dundonald
Belfast BT16 0AN, Northern Ireland

Typeset by Techniset Typesetters, Newton-le-Willows, Merseyside

Printed in Ireland by ColourBooks Limited

A CIP catalogue record for this book is available from the British Library

ISBN 0-85640-610-4

STUFF IT ALL!

A Survivor's Guide to Christmas

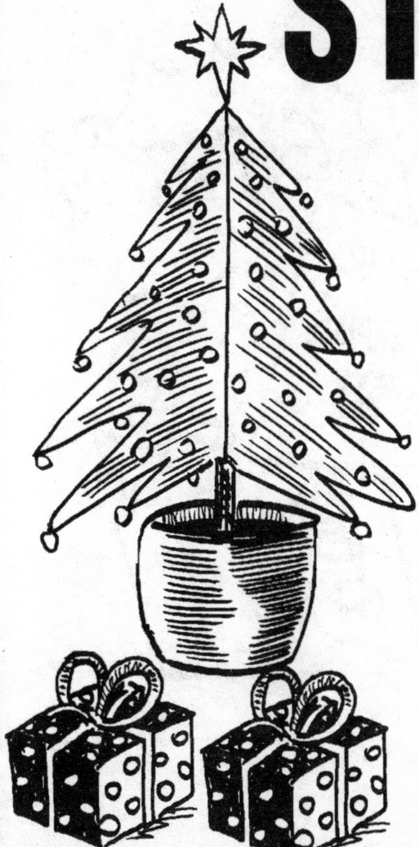

Paul Farrell &
Graeme Keyes

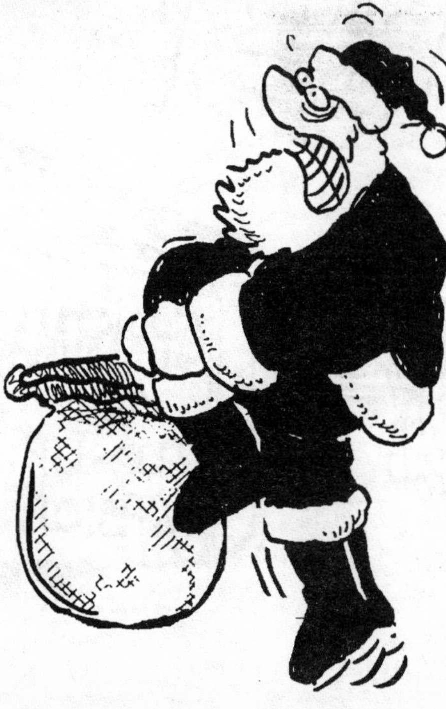

THE
BLACKSTAFF PRESS

BELFAST

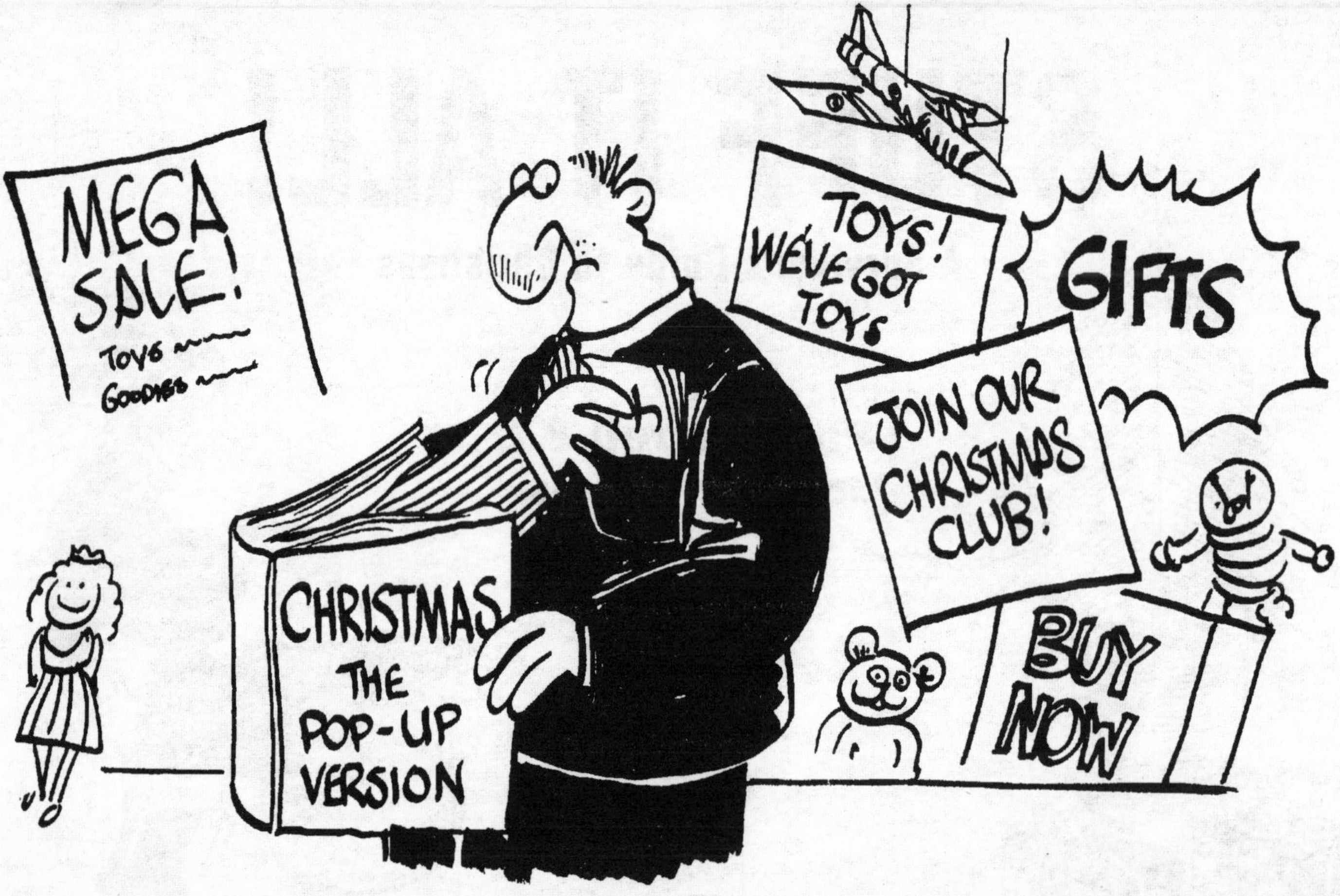
MEGA SALE!
TOYS
GOODIES
TOYS! WE'VE GOT TOYS
GIFTS
JOIN OUR CHRISTMAS CLUB!
CHRISTMAS THE POP-UP VERSION
BUY NOW

Alan Shearer's Game Plan for Christmas Shopping

It is essential to understand that Christmas shopping is a marathon, not a sprint, and all players must be in prime condition. Keeping fit can make the difference between success and failure – between getting your hands on Buzz Lightyear or not!

Training should begin in early autumn and by mid-November you should have started to take shape. The secret is to keep it simple; focus on your goal and never listen to armchair pundits – those catalogue shoppers who order the goods from the comfort of their own homes and seek out products 'not currently available in the shops'. TV shopping is as close as they will ever get to live action – what would they know about real pressure?

Before all away trips study the floor plan of the major stores and watch out for potential pitfalls – the slow lift or troublesome cash register. Homework will pay off in the early games before other shoppers get to know your style and attempt to combat it, but, by then, you should be in the clear. Most own goals come from taking your eye off the ball.

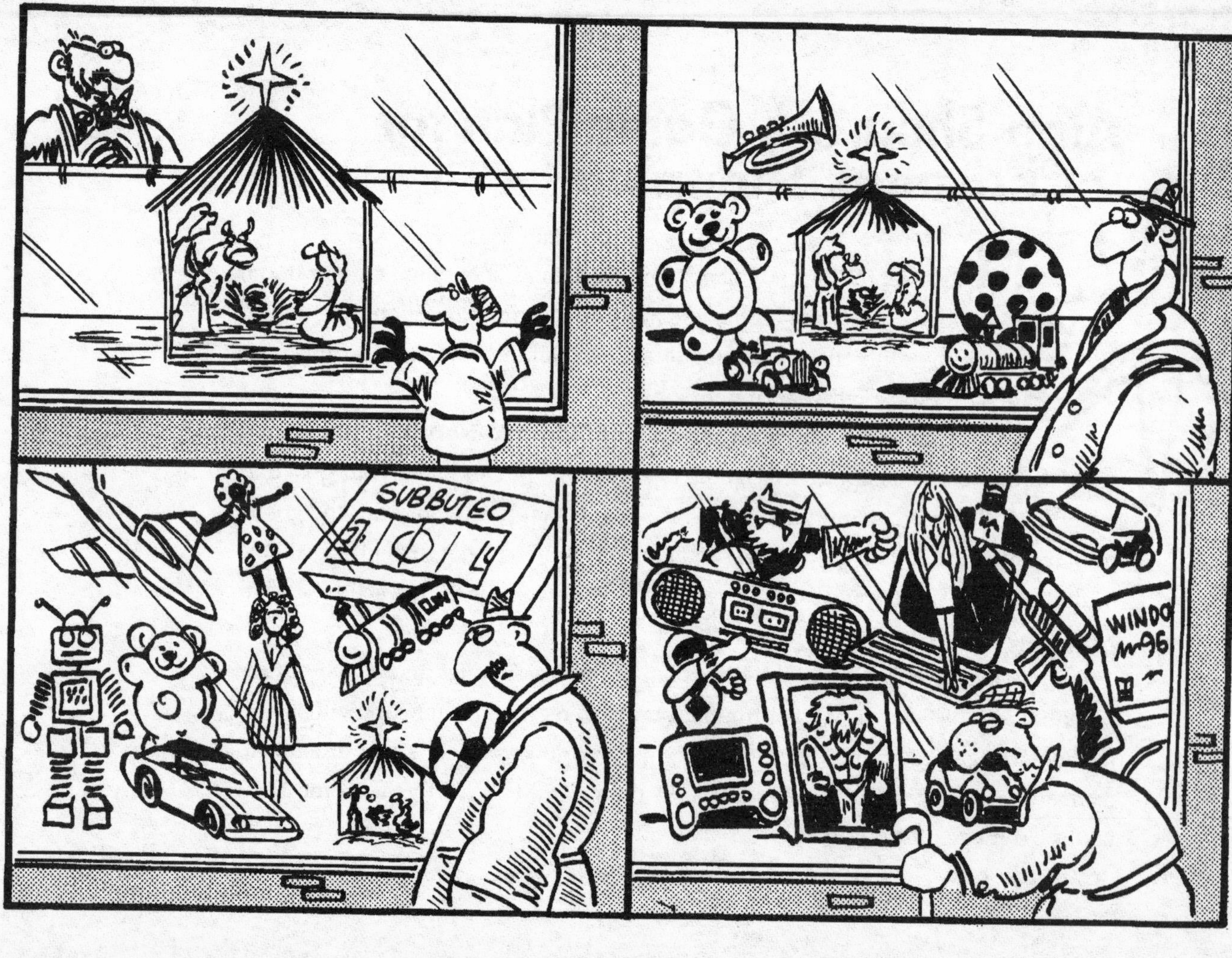
SUBBUTEO
WINDO
96

Large cash reserves can bring the top names within your grasp and enable you to build up an attractive selection, which will also get you through any breakage crisis mid-season. However, avoid introducing costly foreign signings, which may look good on the shop floor but which fail to deliver when the wrapping paper is removed. This is often known as the Middlesbrough Syndrome.

Take it one purchase at a time – at the end of the season they all add up. Pressurise slow shoppers. It's often very effective to unsettle them with taunts of 'dodgy shopper' or 'you'll never shop for England'. Man-to-man marking is another effective strategy and it is important to spot the opposition star shoppers early and take them out before they make too many purchases.

Use the wide open spaces of the larger stores to indulge in stylish shopping techniques – the one-handed pick-up, etc. – but don't go overboard. In smaller, compact shops, the timing of the run is more important and it will be necessary to use the elbow, the shoulder and, if necessary, the knee to create space for shopping. This is where passion will be essential and those months of physical training will finally pay off.

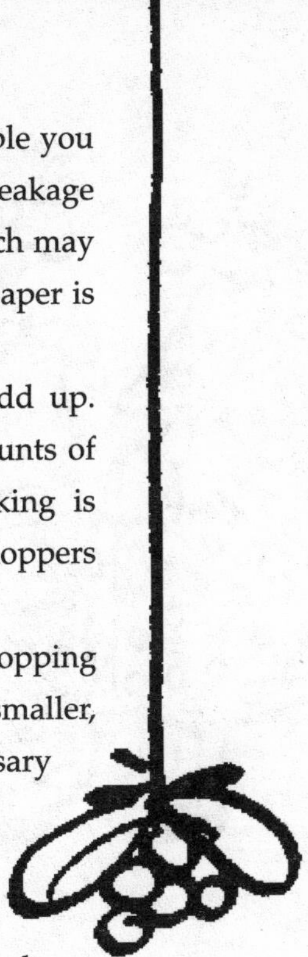

Children's toy departments are notoriously intimidating environments and even the best-prepared shoppers can be caught off guard by the sheer noise and intensity of colour. There is nothing to prepare you for this and experience is your

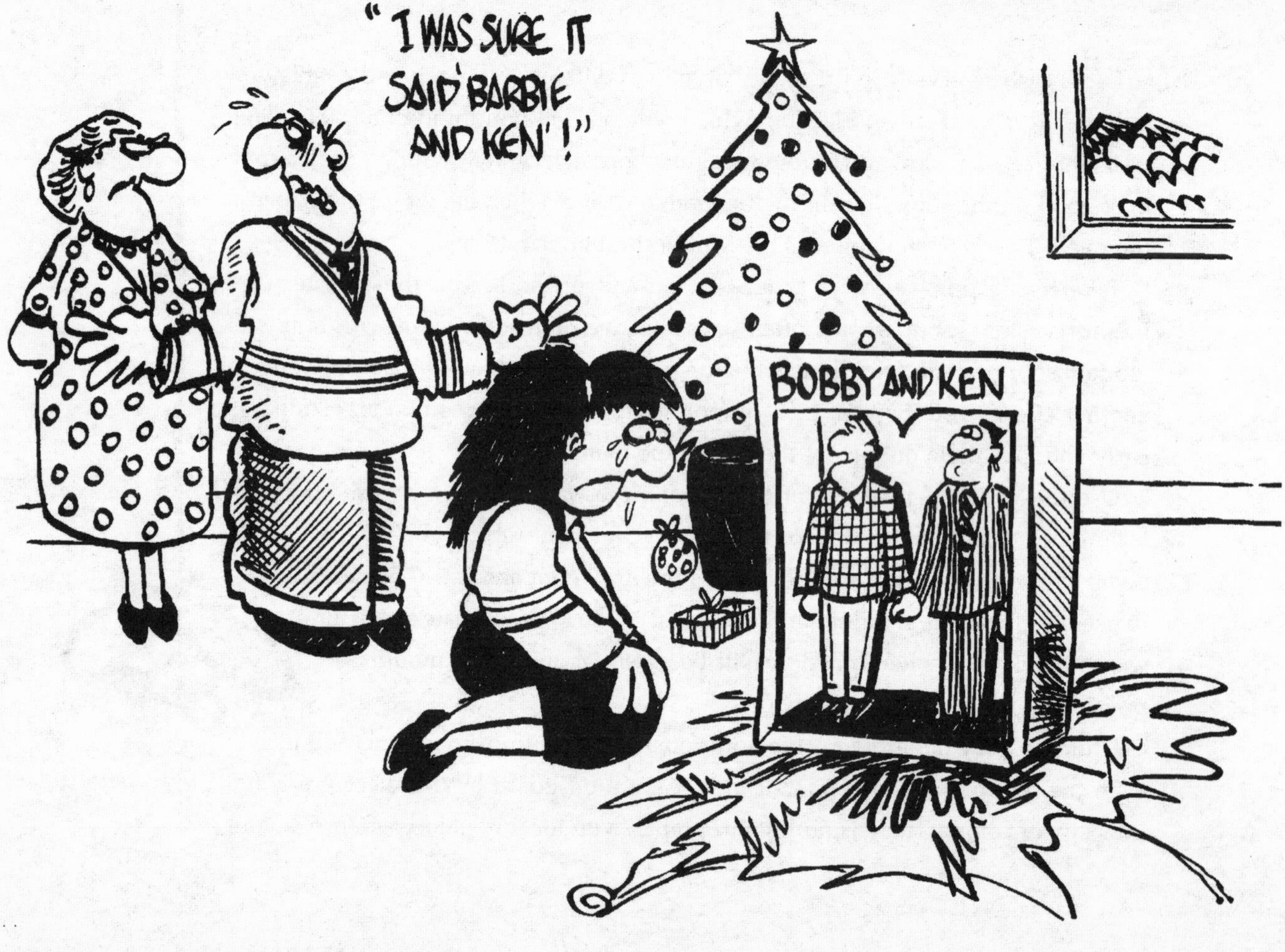
"I WAS SURE IT SAID 'BARBIE AND KEN'!"
BOBBY AND KEN

only advantage, although an early score (such as a quick video game purchase, with batteries included) may settle the nerves before any damage is done.

The real problems, however, surface in the heady atmosphere of the perfume/aftershave counters. The unsuspecting shopper can be assailed by such a frenzy of unfamiliar foreign scents that the game plan goes out the window and, by the end of the fray, all they are left with is a finish that will render them as sick as a parrot. Only by keeping the nose very tight and playing it safe can you guarantee a result here.

Stamina is all important and the December 25th break should be used to recharge all batteries before heading into the post-Christmas sales, where, as any serious shopper knows, some valuable points can be picked up. A good performance now could ensure lucrative qualification for Europe and the potential to bring home some duty-free silverware.

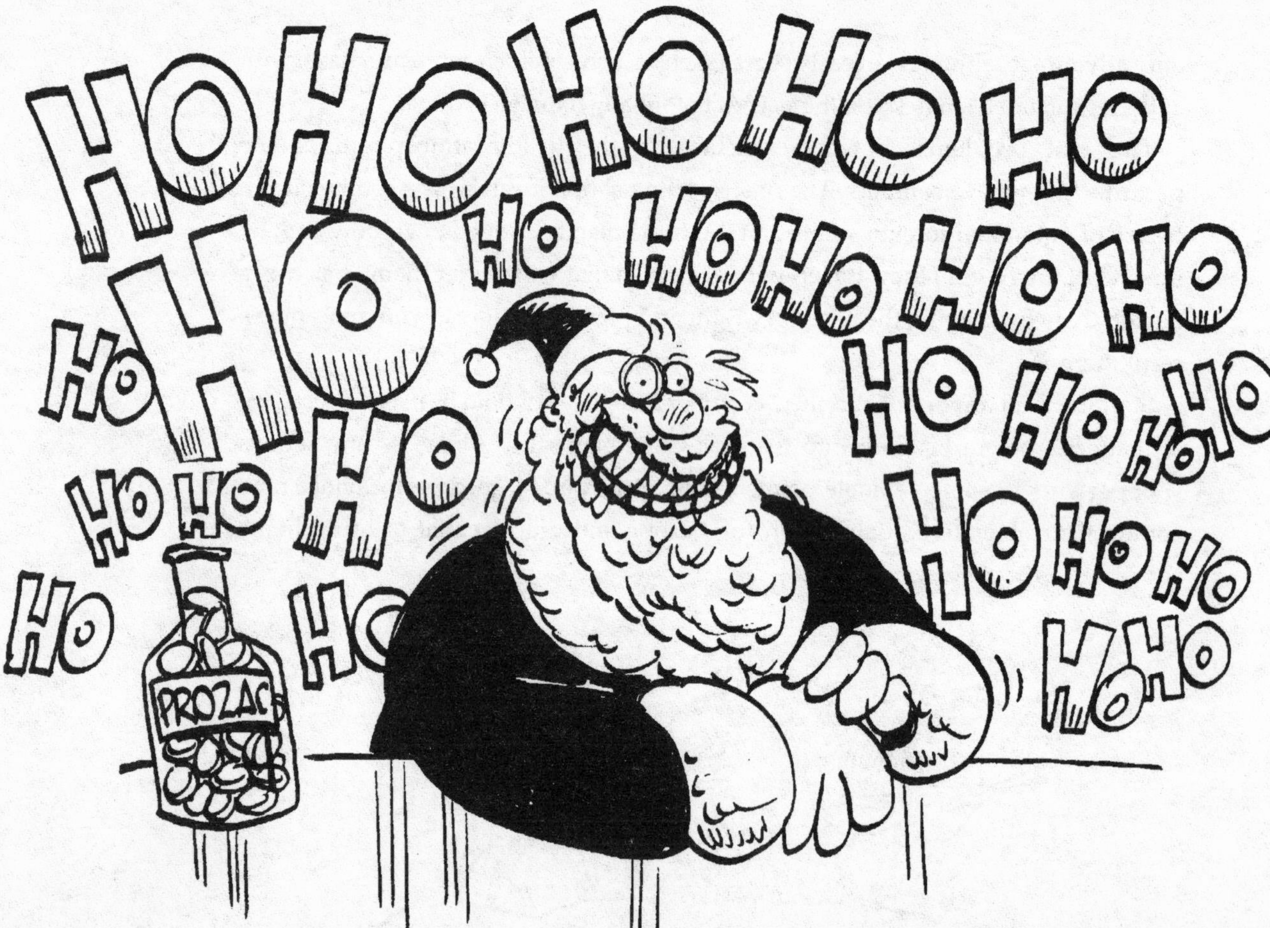
HO HO HO HO HO HO
HO HO HO HO HO HO HO
HO HO HO HO HO HO
HO HO HO HO HO HO HO HO
HO HO HO HO HO HO HO HO
PROZAC

The Real Santa Claus

As a child Santa Claus was not the happiest of little boys because his name, even in Toyland, is considered odd and something of a girlie name. Indeed, the name 'Santa' has never caught on, even in the northern reaches of Scandinavia where they think 'Sven' is quite a cool name.

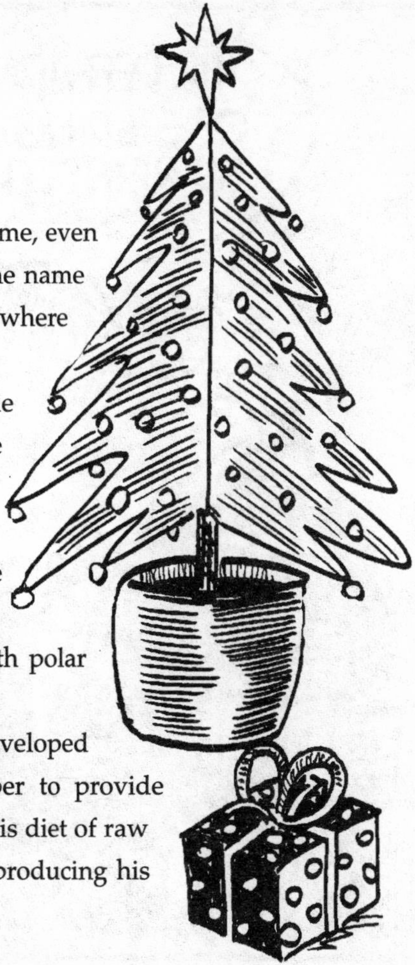

Only among the elves of Toyland did Santa feel comfortable. It is a little known fact that elves have very stupid names themselves and they believe that 'Santa' sounds quite macho. Typical elf names include Fifi Trixibell, Peaches, and Heavenly Hirani Tiger Lily. Most of Santa's formative years were spent playing entirely with elves, which removed him from the sphere of adult influence, and, like Michael Jackson, he is now more at home with children than with grown-ups. He is also more at home with polar bears than with grown-ups, but this is because he lives in the North Pole.

The harsh climate has also had an effect on Santa and he has developed physically much like the whale, building up large supplies of blubber to provide insulation and energy during the freezing winter and freezing summer. His diet of raw fish, while bland, is nevertheless healthy and good for his complexion, producing his

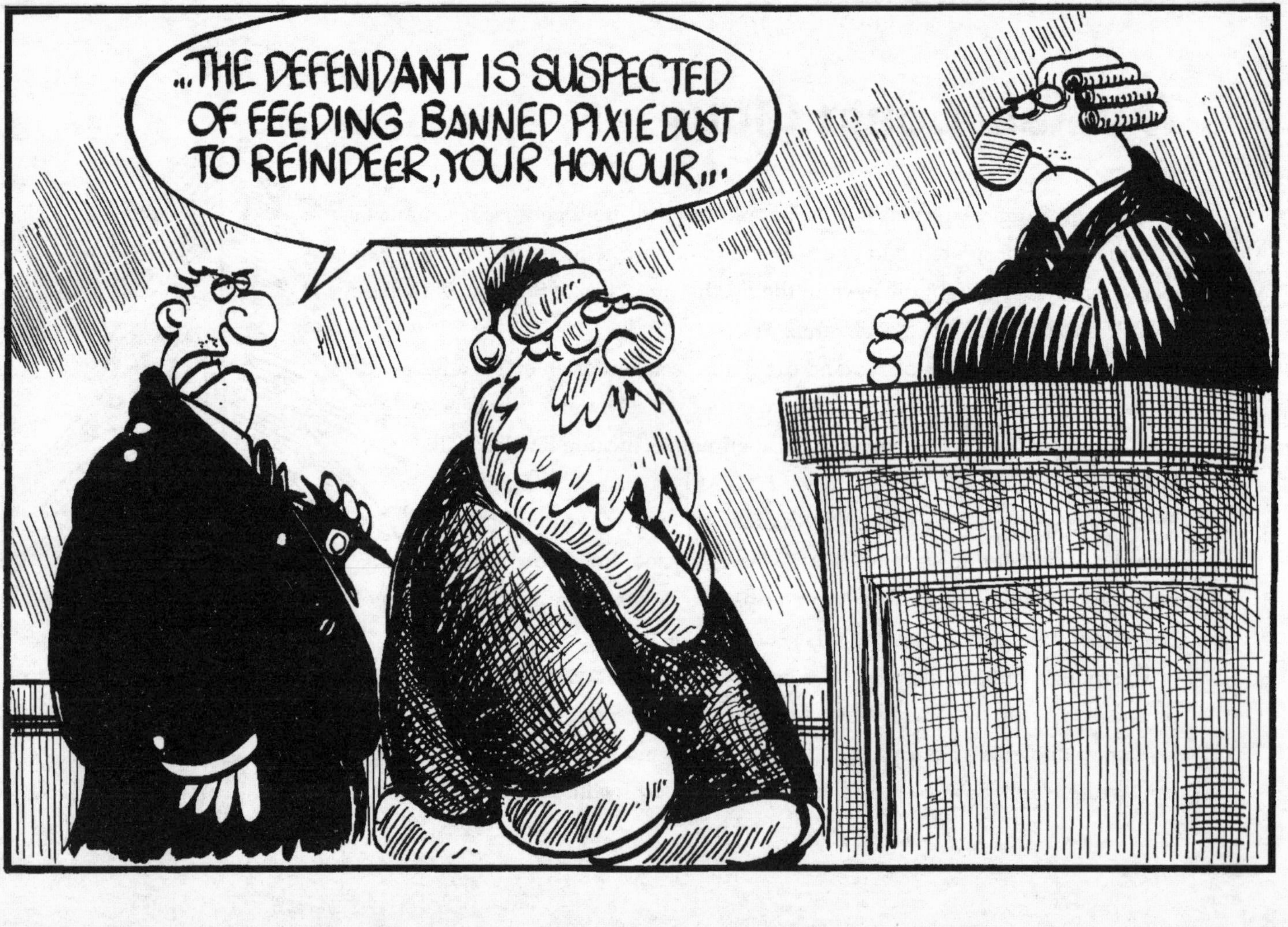
...THE DEFENDANT IS SUSPECTED OF FEEDING BANNED PIXIE DUST TO REINDEER, YOUR HONOUR...

rosy cheeks and the incredible stamina required to travel around the world at supersonic speeds. However, he is also a big fan of Pot Noodles.

From a fashion point of view, Santa is obviously a firm believer in red, which, he says, never goes out of fashion. He has four identical outfits – red polar bear fur with a white polar bear trim. Polar bears are used, as lambs are in short supply in this part of the world, and one skinned adult polar bear will provide enough material for four outfits (XL), a nice rug and twelve pairs of mittens. When it comes to footwear, black seal skin boots are Santa's trademark, because sandals, moccasins, etc., while certainly attractive, prove unsuitable for the subzero climate.

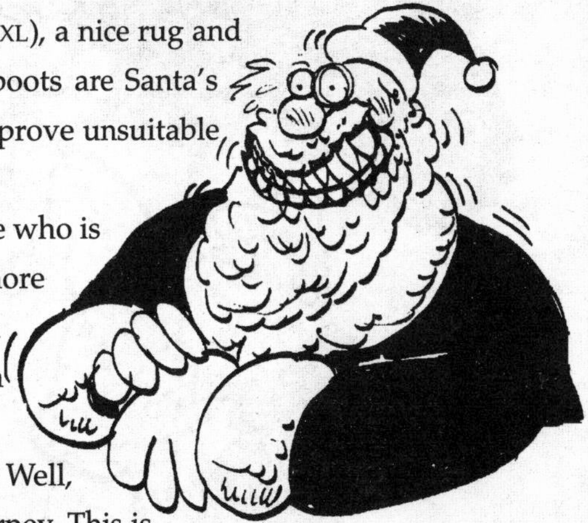

Santa's choice of lurid red, however, seems a strange one for someone who is determined not to be seen at night. Surely black would be a more appropriate choice? But Santa prefers red – he says black makes his bum look big – and, anyway, a single trip down the chimney renders him effectively invisible for the rest of the night.

So what does a man who tours one day a year do with his spare time? Well, he has to keep fit in preparation for his challenging Christmas Eve journey. This is done in three ways: reindeer lifting, reindeer wrestling and reindeer jumping – all of which are self-explanatory. Animal rights groups may have reservations about some of these practices.

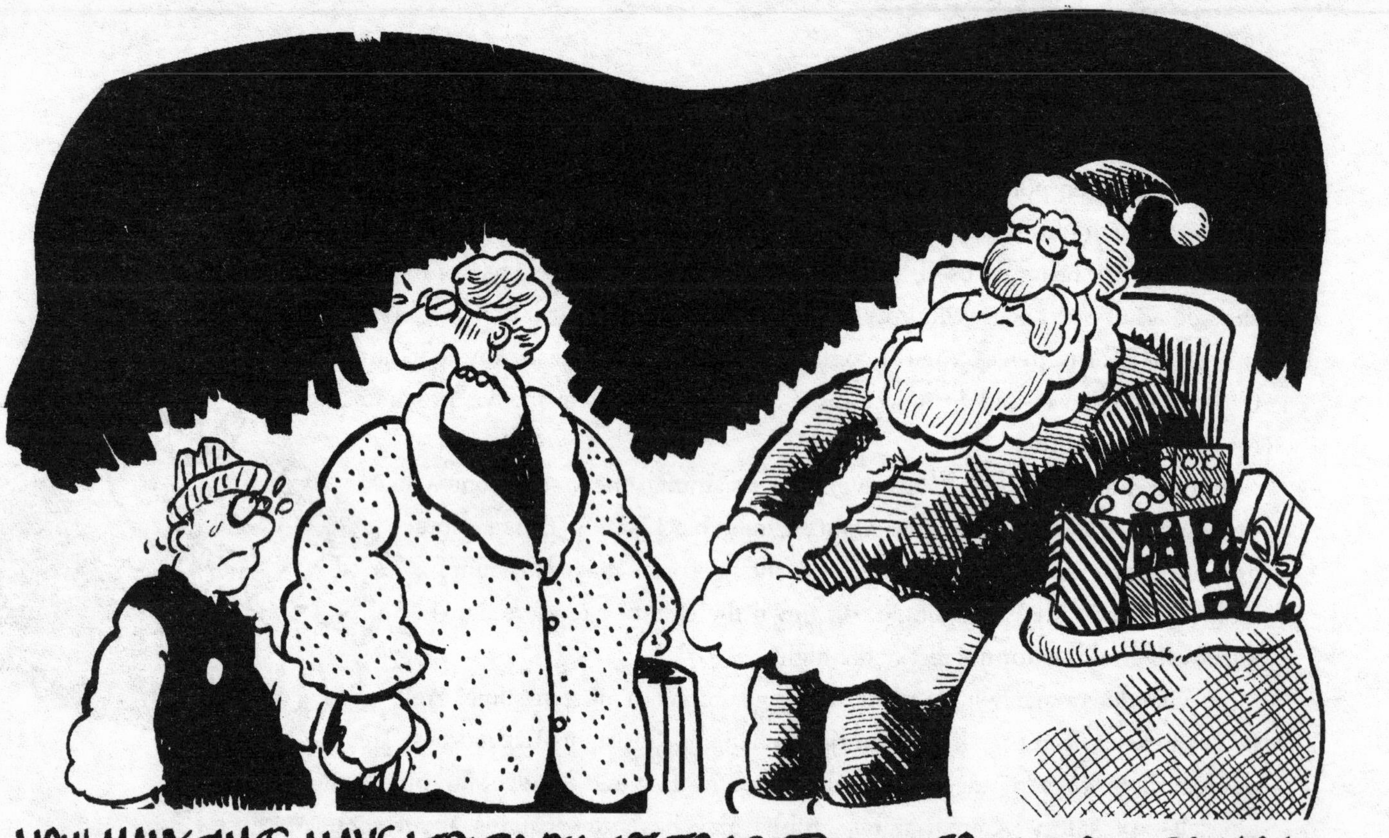

HOW MANY TIMES HAVE I TOLD YOU NOT TO ACCEPT GIFTS FROM STRANGE MEN!

Part of his very long day – it is daylight for six months in the North Pole – is taken up with running the shop floor of the massive toy manufacturing plant. Santa is a hard task master who does not believe in unions, which, he claims, would jeopardise the smooth running of Toyland. Certainly manufacturing enough toys for all the good Christian children in the world is a daunting undertaking and the elves work long hours for little pay. A little-known organisation called the Elf Liberation Front (ELF) has previously caused problems through industrial sabotage, but, so far, they have failed to bring about reform.

These are difficult times for elves generally, with the trend in children's toys leaning heavily towards computer and video games. If this continues, Santa will eventually be forced to introduce new technology into his Toyland workshops, necessitating the laying-off of large numbers of staff who will find themselves living on social elfare.

However, not all elves have it so tough and the lucky ones get to work in Santa's huge postal sorting office, where millions of soot-stained letters arrive every day, especially from mid-November. Many elves are employed to open these letters and sort them – spotting those from naughty children, non-Christians or adults – and due to the variety of languages, there are hundreds of highly paid elf translators employed on a consultancy basis. The letters are

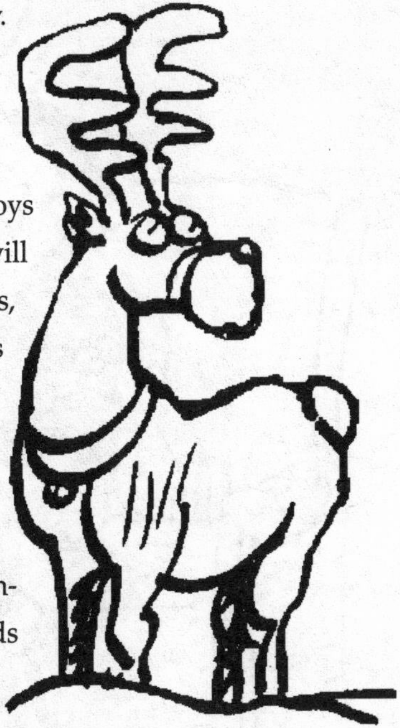

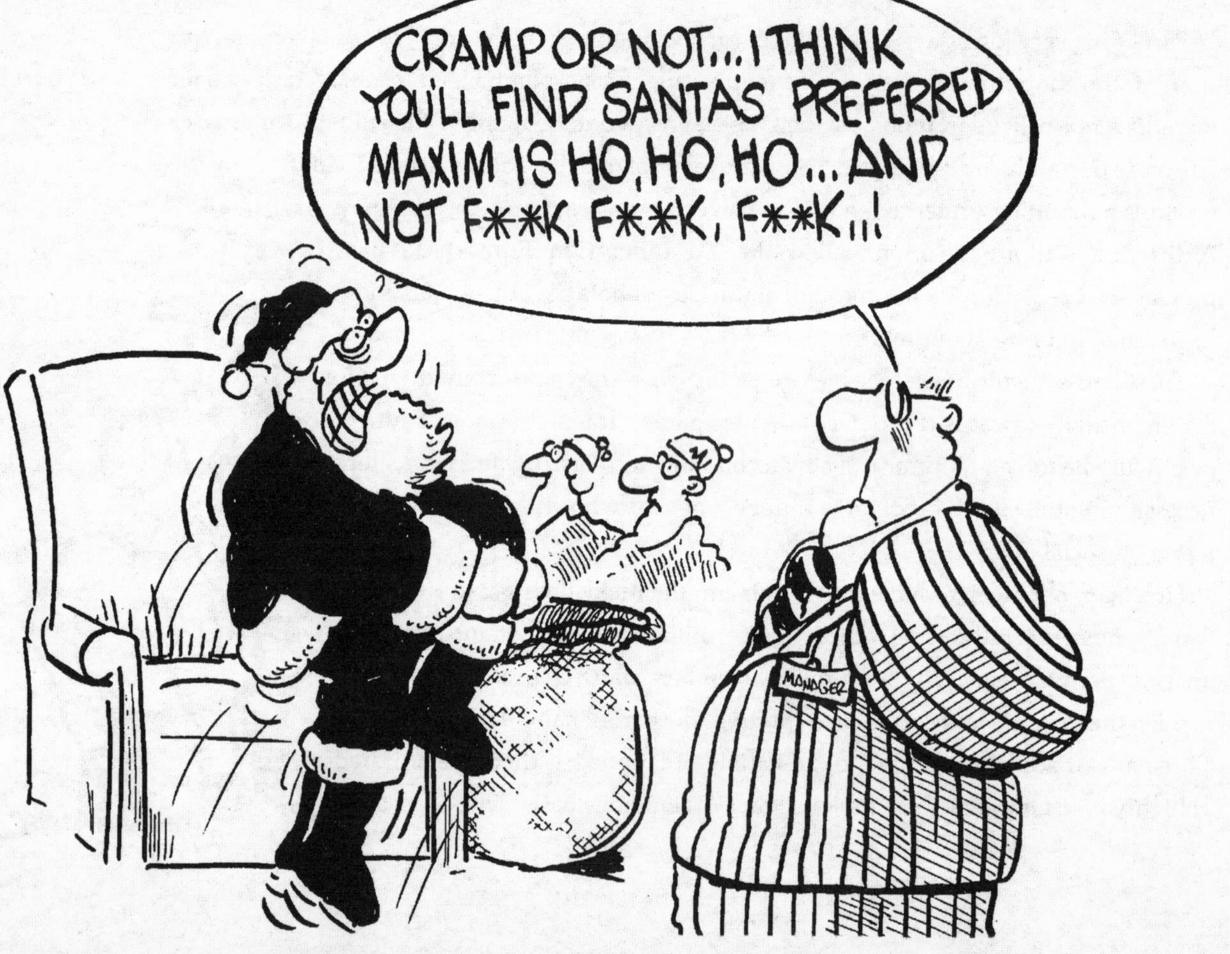
CRAMP OR NOT... I THINK YOU'LL FIND SANTA'S PREFERRED MAXIM IS HO, HO, HO... AND NOT F**K, F**K, F**K...!
MANAGER

collected by intrepid post-elves who travel all around the world, constantly at risk from cats, magpies and other predators. As a result, they are all trained in the art of elf-defence.

At the end of the day Santa likes nothing better than to put his feet up and watch a video while sipping a snowball or two. His favourite movie is *Miracle on 34th Street* (the 1947 version), which, he believes, has come closest to capturing on screen the real essence of his personality. He also has a thing about Maureen O'Hara.

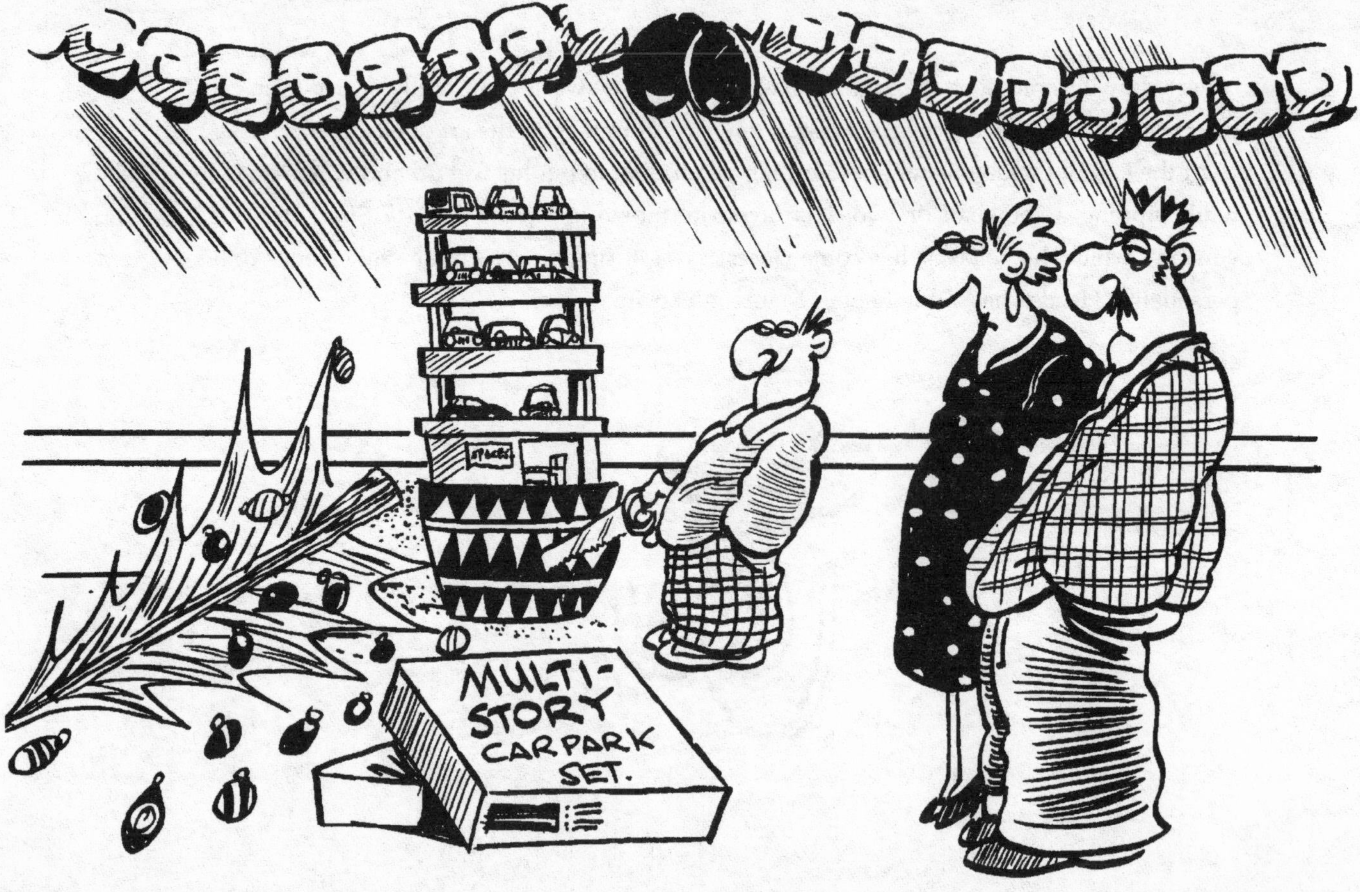
MULTI-
STORY
CAR PARK
SET.

Dear Santa

The postal division of Santa's Toyland operation is hugely labour intensive and there is little time for personal service. 'Difficult' letters are often 'mislaid' by overworked elves, leaving the writer to receive Santa's standard package – a sort of to-whom-it-may-concern delivery from Toyland, which rarely includes any of the most sought-after toys. Top toys are always allocated to those children who specifically request them and are consigned in order of legibility, punctuality and behaviour over the year. It is not widely known by most children that their behaviour actually rates below their handwriting skill in Santa's eyes but, as in adult life, it is not being good that matters but being seen to be good.

How to guarantee success
Handwriting
Santa has realised that it is not easy to accurately rate whether children have truly been good or bad without highly detailed psychological research and intensive behavioural analysis over a long period in a confined environment – something that

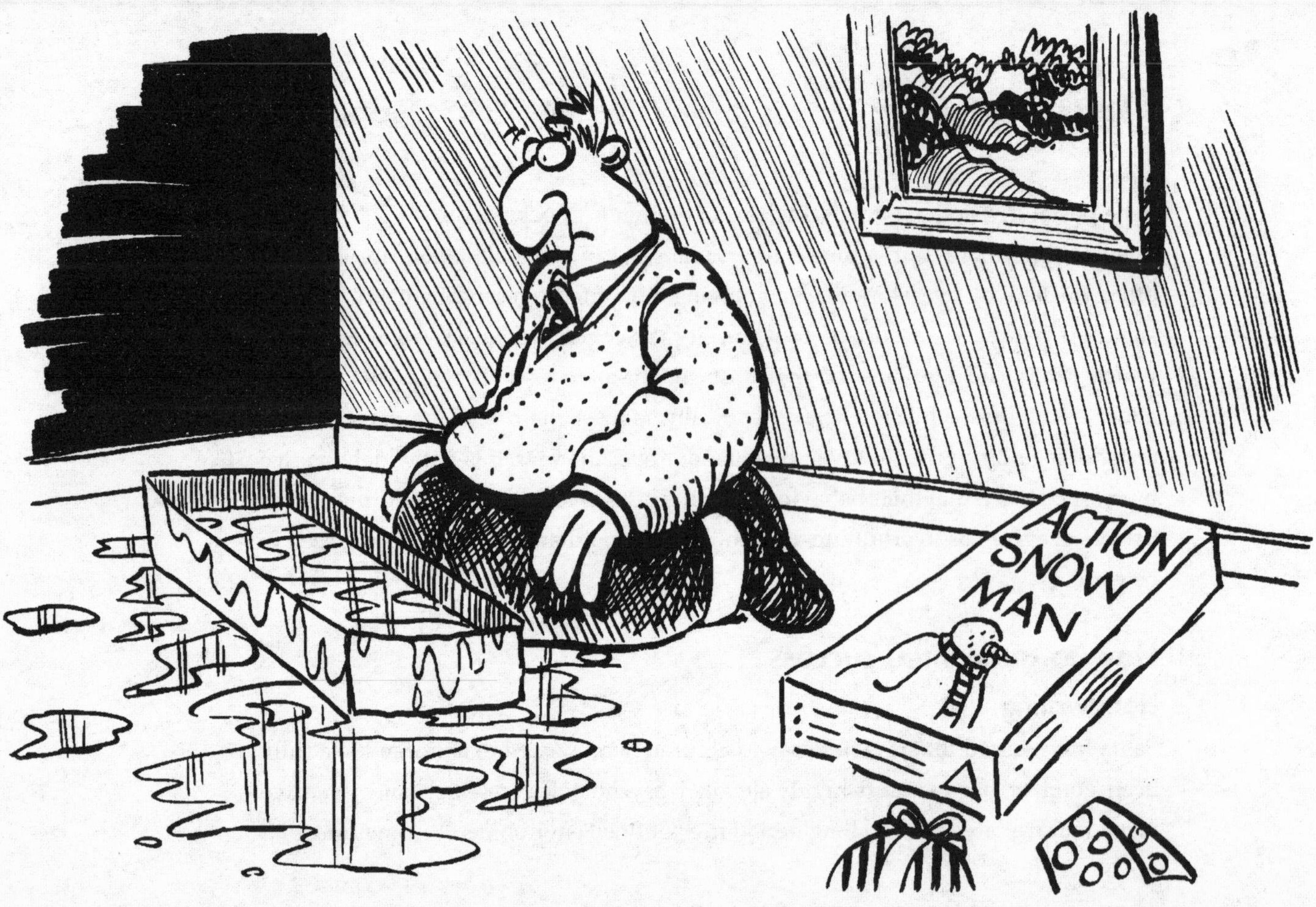
ACTION
SNOW
MAN

is prohibited by the constitutions of most countries. As a result, he has adopted the handwriting test which can effectively be summed up as follows: legible is good; illegible is bad. It is recommended that children who are serious about getting their toys either use a word processor or get their parents to write their letters. On no account should crayons be used – they may be cute but elves in Santa's sorting office consider them to be evidence of evil.

Punctuality

The letter should always be put up the chimney by mid-November to ensure collection by the local post-elf on his early round. However, if it is put up too early, it may end up covered in soot and not be discovered. (This is also why black envelopes are considered a bad idea.) If the letter misses the first collection, it may not arrive in Toyland until mid-December, by which time most of the popular toys will have been allocated and Santa will be left with the jigsaws, colouring sets and items of clothing.

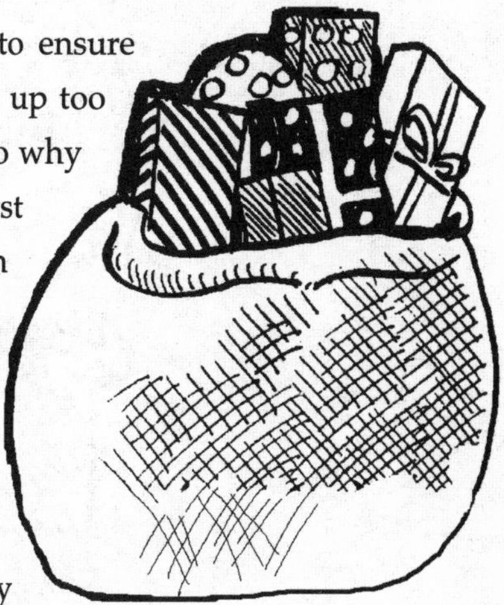

Style

Always start the letter with the phrase 'Dear Santa'. Do not try to be different or clever, as such individuality will be screened out by the highly

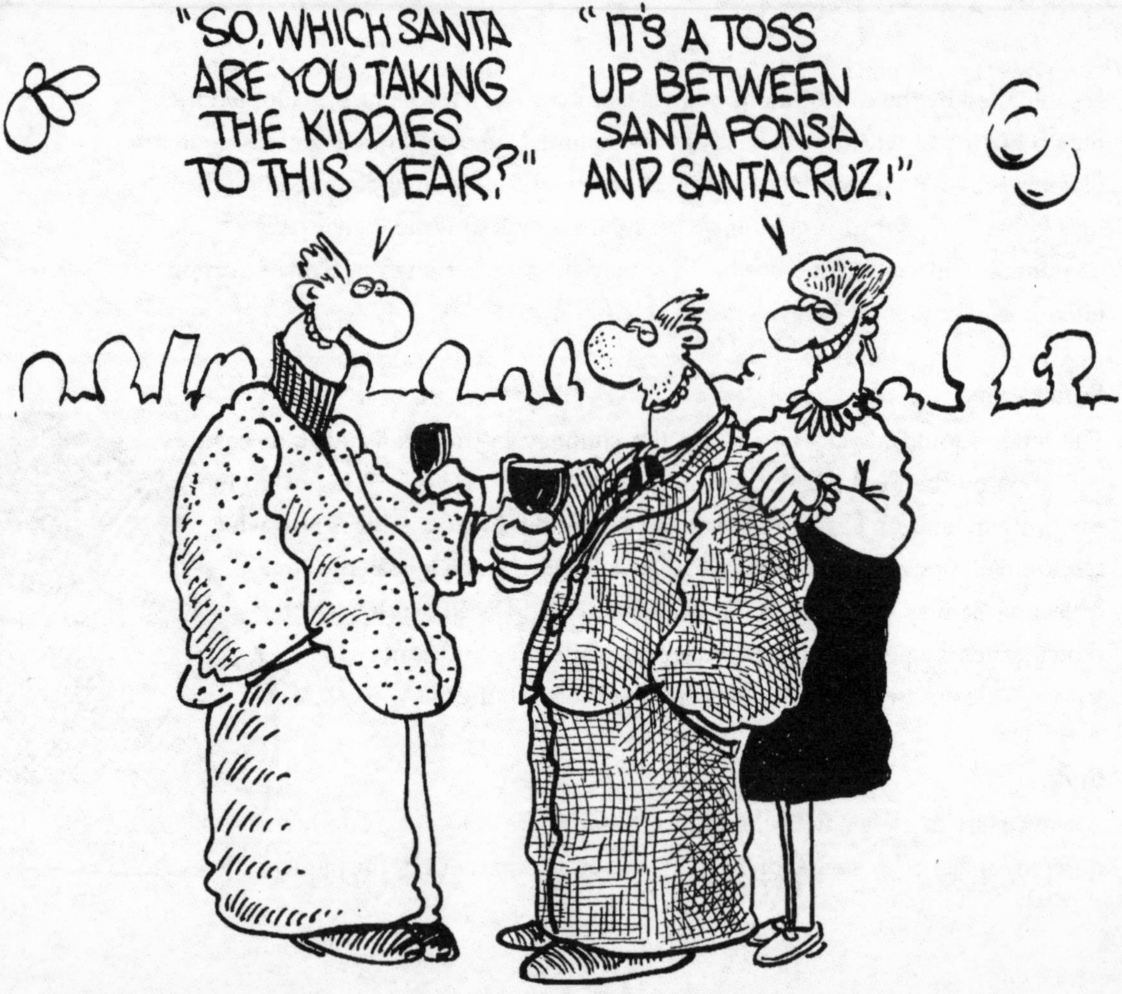
"SO, WHICH SANTA ARE YOU TAKING THE KIDDIES TO THIS YEAR?"
"IT'S A TOSS UP BETWEEN SANTA PONSA AND SANTA CRUZ!"

conservative sorting elves. Appellations such as 'Daddy-o', 'Big-man', 'Fatso', 'Old-timer', 'Friend of the Eskimo', etc., will result in immediate rejection, as will any letters containing either bribes or the promise of bribes. While there were rumours in the late '60s of corruption among Santa's sorting elves – alleging that they placed certain letters at the top of the pile in return for chocolate-coated peanuts – an investigation failed to uncover any real proof. A subsequent restructuring of the division was, nevertheless, carried out, which saw some senior elves 'moved sideways'.

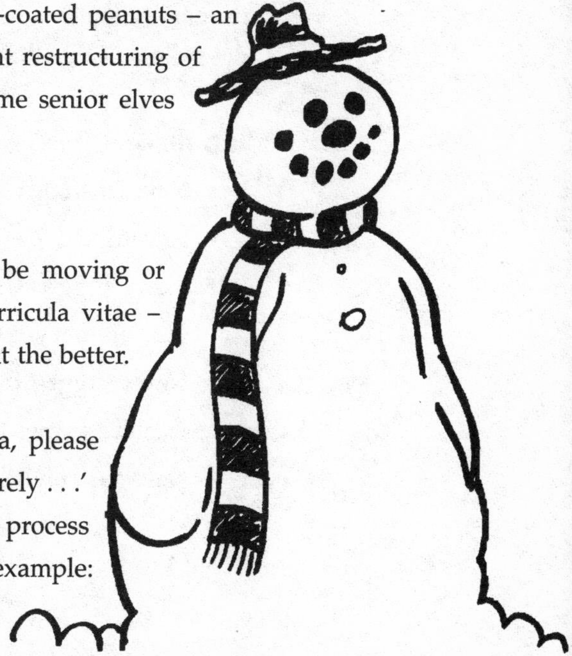

Be concise

Letters to Santa are not essays and are not expected to be moving or stimulating. In Toyland they are considered much like curricula vitae – sources of information – and like CVs, the less embellishment the better. Always keep the letter to one page and use a list format.

The most effective formula is the following: 'Dear Santa, please forward the following items to the undersigned. Yours sincerely . . .' This letter style is appreciated by the sorting elves who can process the document with ease. Contrast it with the following example: 'Dearest Santa, I have been a very good boy / girl all year and

I am really looking forward to Christmas. My mummy was sick at one stage and I looked after her, so I would like a doctor/nurse outfit, etc., etc.' This is the kind of sentimental nonsense that sorting elves abhor and is the equivalent of a ten-page CV which details primary school results and includes 'reading and going to the theatre' as hobbies.

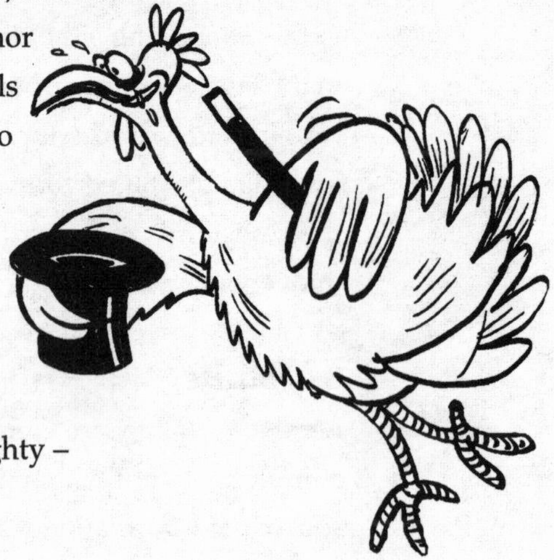

Top tips

- Never include a photograph of yourself.
- Never include a photograph of anybody else.
- Never suggest that the kid next door has been naughty – you will not get some of his/her toys.
- Never suggest that you are poor – children of the wealthy always get more toys.
- Never use invisible ink.

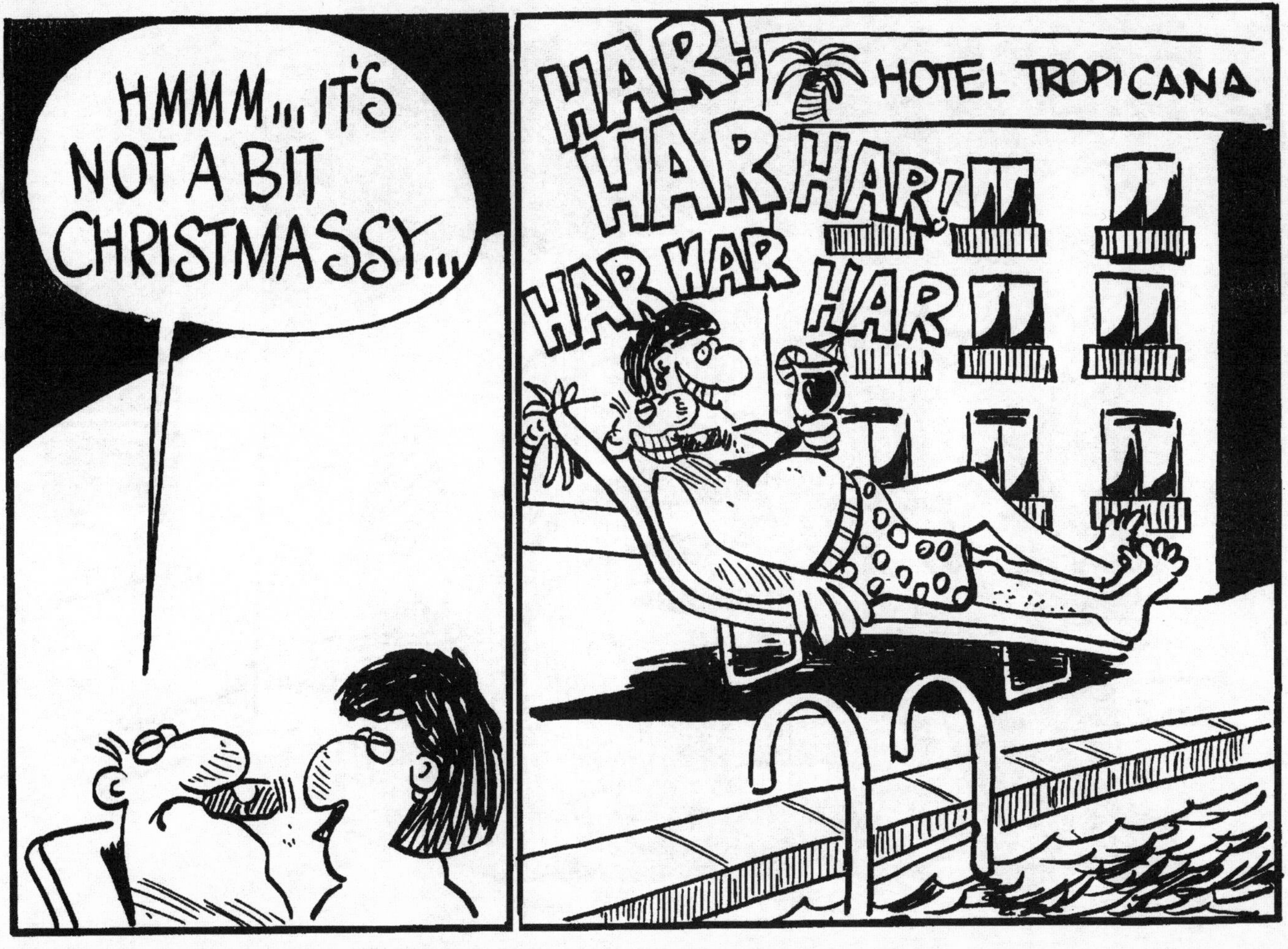
HMMM... IT'S NOT A BIT CHRISTMASSY...
HAR! HAR HAR HAR! HAR HAR HAR
HOTEL TROPICANA

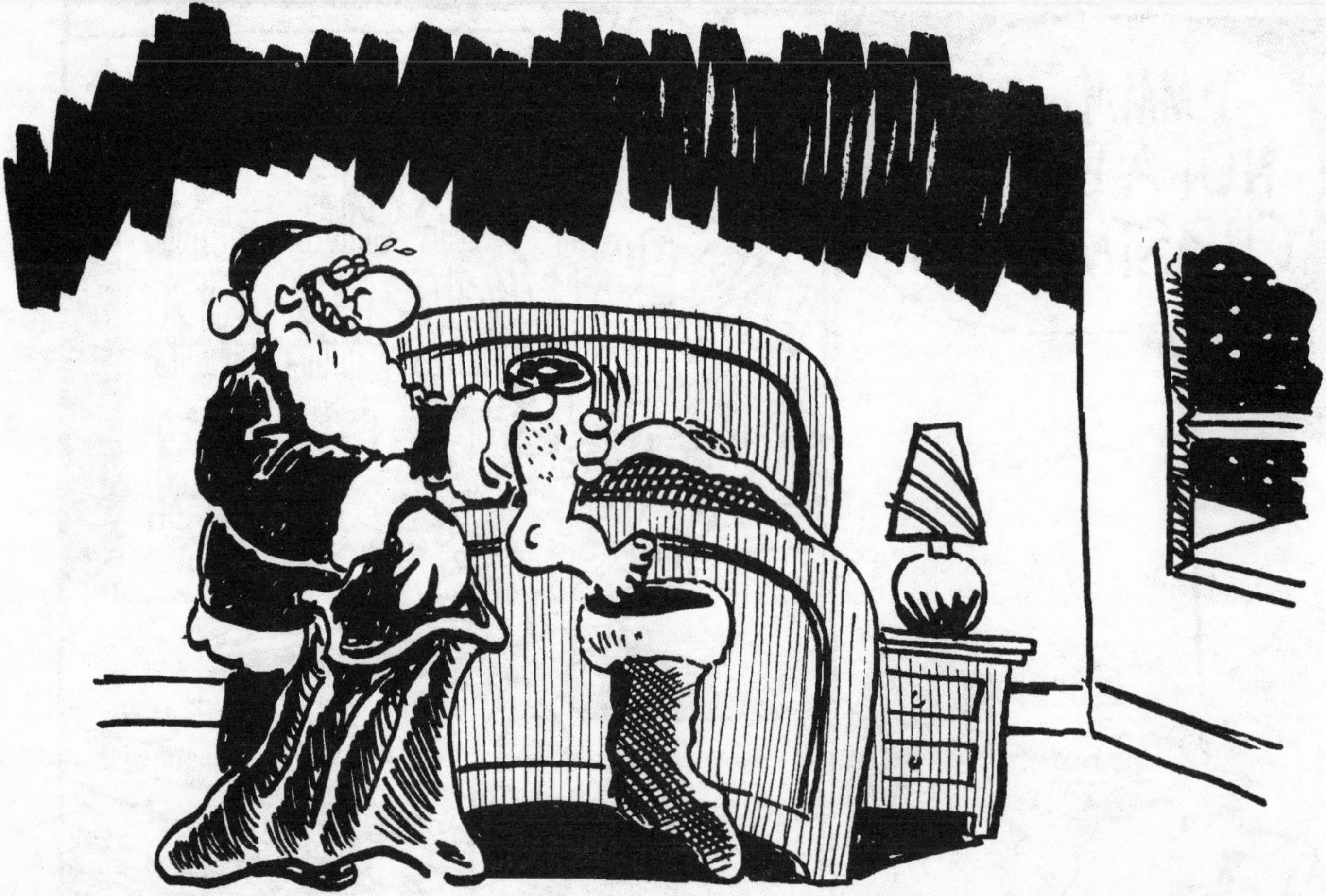

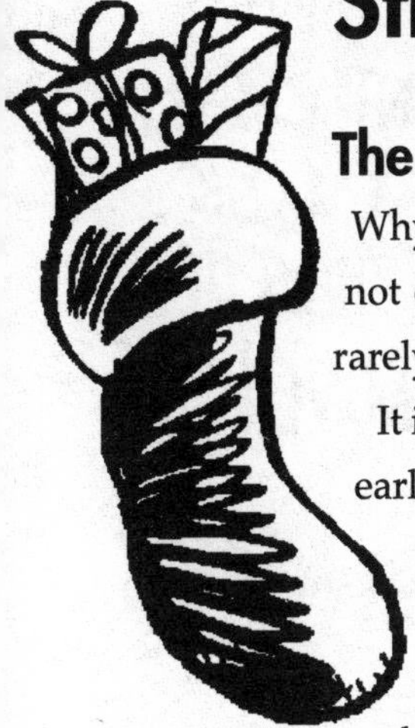

Strange Christmas Traditions

The Christmas stocking

Why should Santa Claus leave presents in stockings? The shape of the stocking is not one which lends itself to maximum usage of space and, ordinarily, items are rarely packed in stocking-shaped containers, including stockings.

It is thought that this tradition started when Italian stocking manufacturers in the early nineteenth century were desperate to increase sales and an advertising agency targeted the Christmas market with the slogan, 'Let Santa into your stockings' – considered shocking at the time. This controversial Benetton campaign was eventually banned but the message stuck and even with the advent of tights, stockings are still hung out on Christmas Eve all around the world. A subsequent Benetton campaign – 'Let Santa fill your knickers' – failed to have the same impact on the Christmas market.

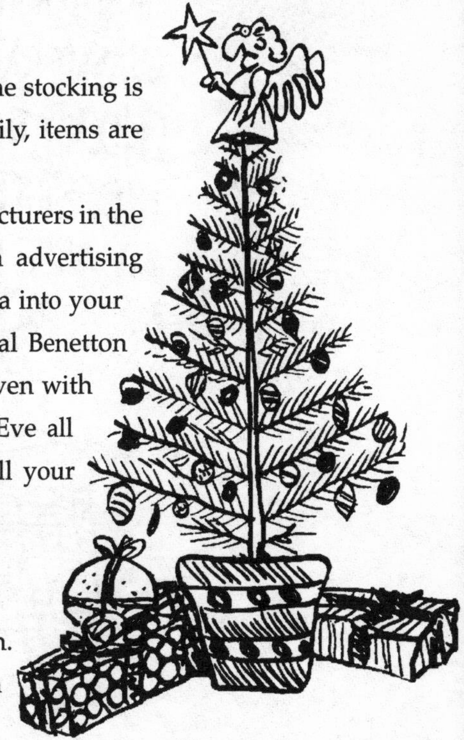

The Christmas tree

Even stranger than the stocking tradition is the Christmas tree tradition. In the latter part of the eighteenth century it was common for each

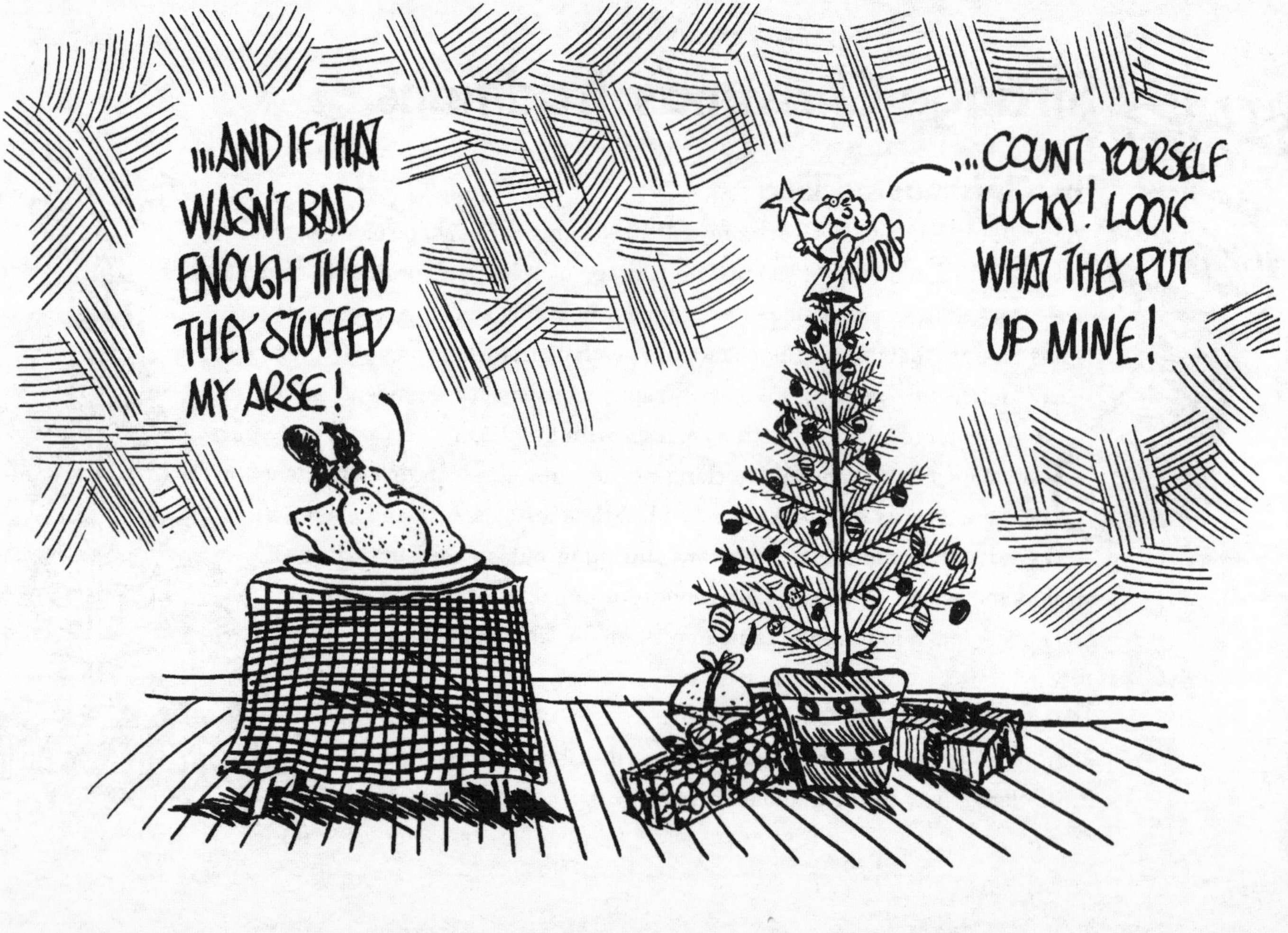
...AND IF THAT WASN'T BAD ENOUGH THEN THEY STUFFED MY ARSE!
...COUNT YOURSELF LUCKY! LOOK WHAT THEY PUT UP MINE!

family to place some coloured paper or string on a bush outside the house to mark the arrival of Christmas. But in Scotland this caused problems because the tight-fisted locals would steal the coloured paper and string and sometimes even the bush itself, rather than fork out for their own materials. As a result, honest Scottish people began to bring their plant life and coloured paper inside in order to foil their mean neighbours.

Strangely, unlike haggis, kilts, tossing the caber and all other Scottish traditions, this particular custom spread to other countries and all around the world Christmas bushes and, later, trees were erected inside the house during the festive season. The coloured paper has since been replaced by electric lights, except in Scotland where the cheaper option of paper is considered a more sensible idea.

The Yule log

Named after its inventor, Yule Brenner, the Yule log is thought to symbolise the lack of hair on the newborn baby Jesus and therefore the unimportance of hair generally. Why the popular follicly challenged Hollywood actor chose a log to represent this is unclear, although the total absence of any leaves may provide a clue.

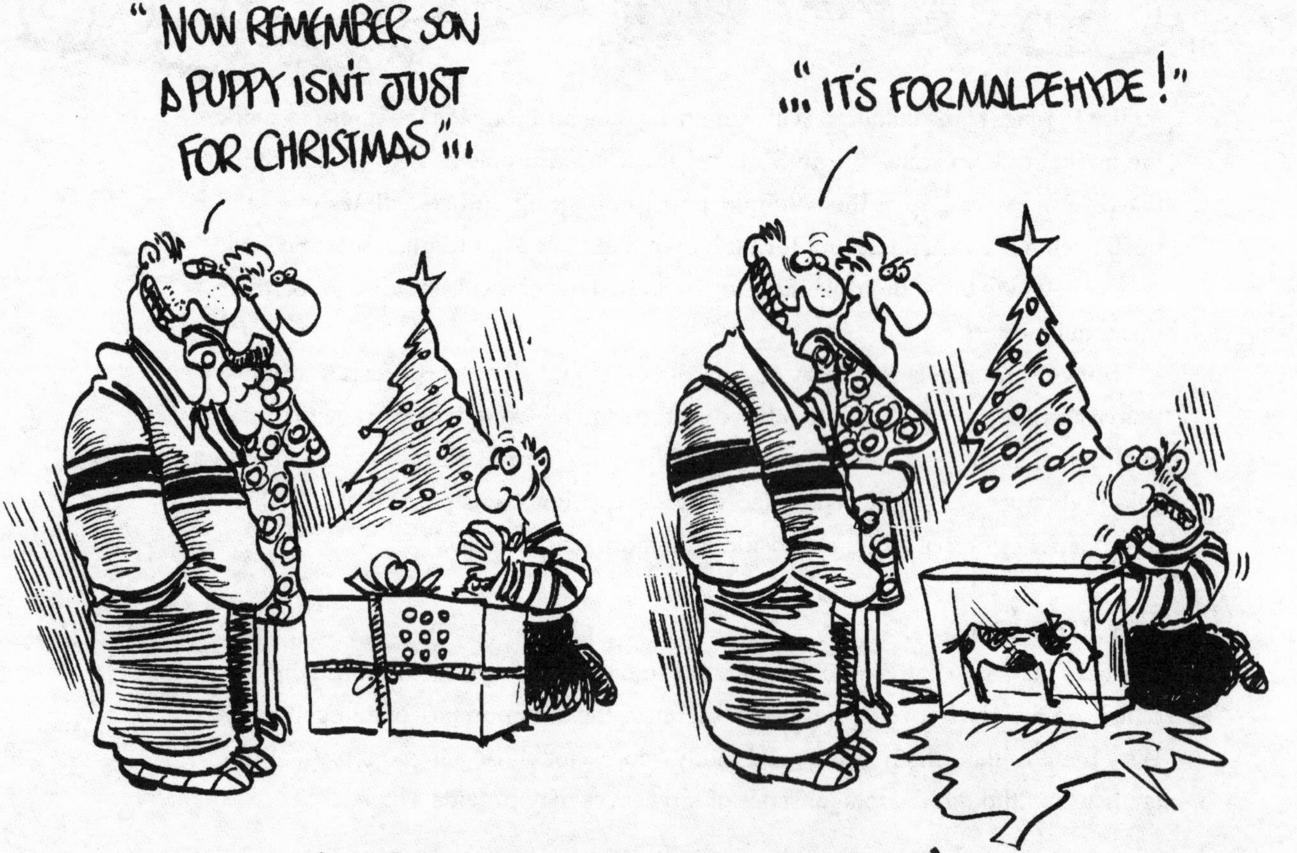
"NOW REMEMBER SON A PUPPY ISN'T JUST FOR CHRISTMAS"...
..."IT'S FORMALDEHYDE!"

(CHRISTMAS WITH THE HIRSTS...)

Holly

Holly's shiny leaves and ability to bear fruit in winter have nothing whatsoever to do with the Christmas tradition. Rather, it is used to symbolise Hollywood – the real heart and soul of Christmas. December is traditionally a hugely profitable time for the major Hollywood studios, which rely on their seasonal blockbusters to ensure a healthy bottom line. Everyone benefits from this Christmas tradition, not least the children who are treated to some real movie gems. The independent film sector, which tends to make less of an impact at Christmas, is represented by ivy because it often makes creepy movies.

Mistletoe

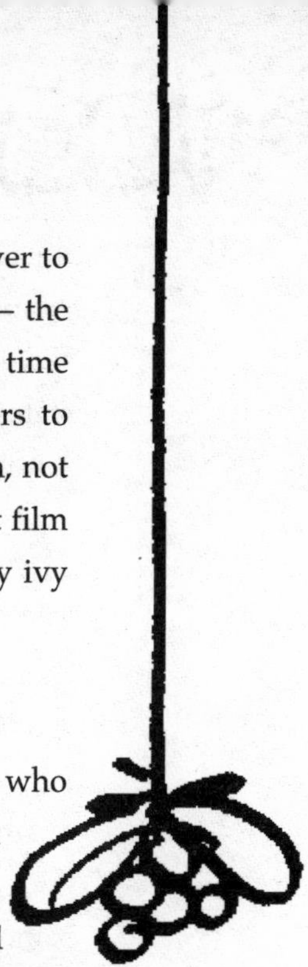

This strange plant was considered a source of magic by the ancient Druids, who never used it as an excuse for a quick snog. This tradition only gathered momentum in the earlier part of this century when a handsome gardener asked a passer-by if she would 'like some mistletoe'. Thinking he had asked her if she would 'like to kiss his toe', she replied, 'No thank you, but I'll kiss your mouth if you like.' The stunned gardener accepted the offer and the pair later moved in together, after he deserted his own wife and young family. Word quickly spread and mistletoe became a symbol for kissing strangers with a view to breaking

up their marriages.

Today mistletoe is very popular at Christmas parties, where it serves much the same purpose as alcohol does throughout the rest of the year. Mistletoe etiquette states that you should never hang a sprig out of your fly and it should be noted that it is not a legally accepted defence in cases of improper behaviour.

The Christmas card

The Christmas card is one of the most visible displays of the season but how this custom began remains a mystery. There is no evidence in the Bible that Jesus received more than his fair share of birthday cards and certainly there is nothing to suggest that his neighbours sent each other cards to celebrate his birthday. Historians have ventured that one birthday card addressed to Jesus, c/o Nazareth, ended up next door and the recipient thought it only polite to respond with the same message, 'Happy Birthday, Christ', to the original sender.

Things would have continued at this rather local level had not young Julius Hallmarcus been around at the time and spotted the potential of such communications. He patented the word 'Christmas', packaged the cards in appealing images of snow – a rare sight in Galilee – and set about amassing a

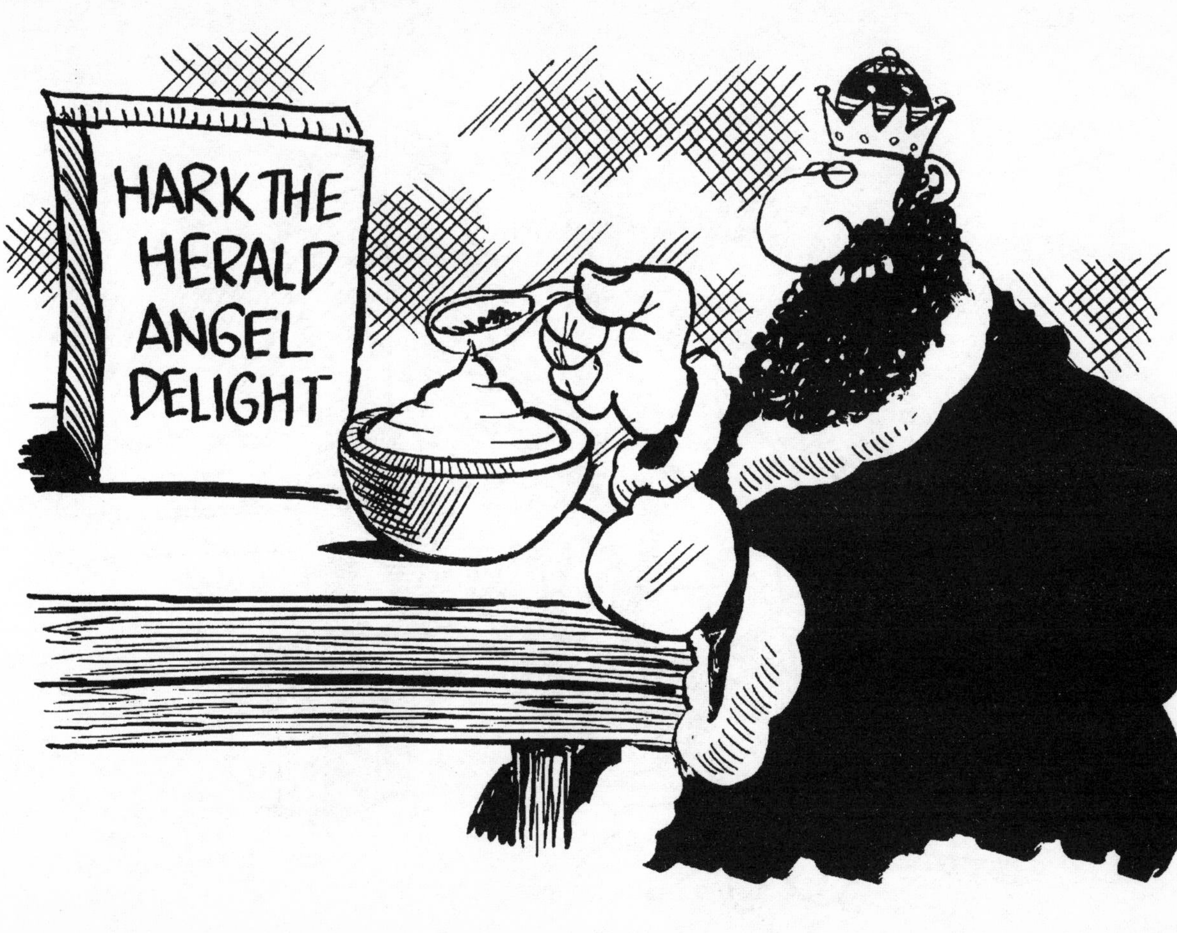
HARK THE
HERALD
ANGEL
DELIGHT

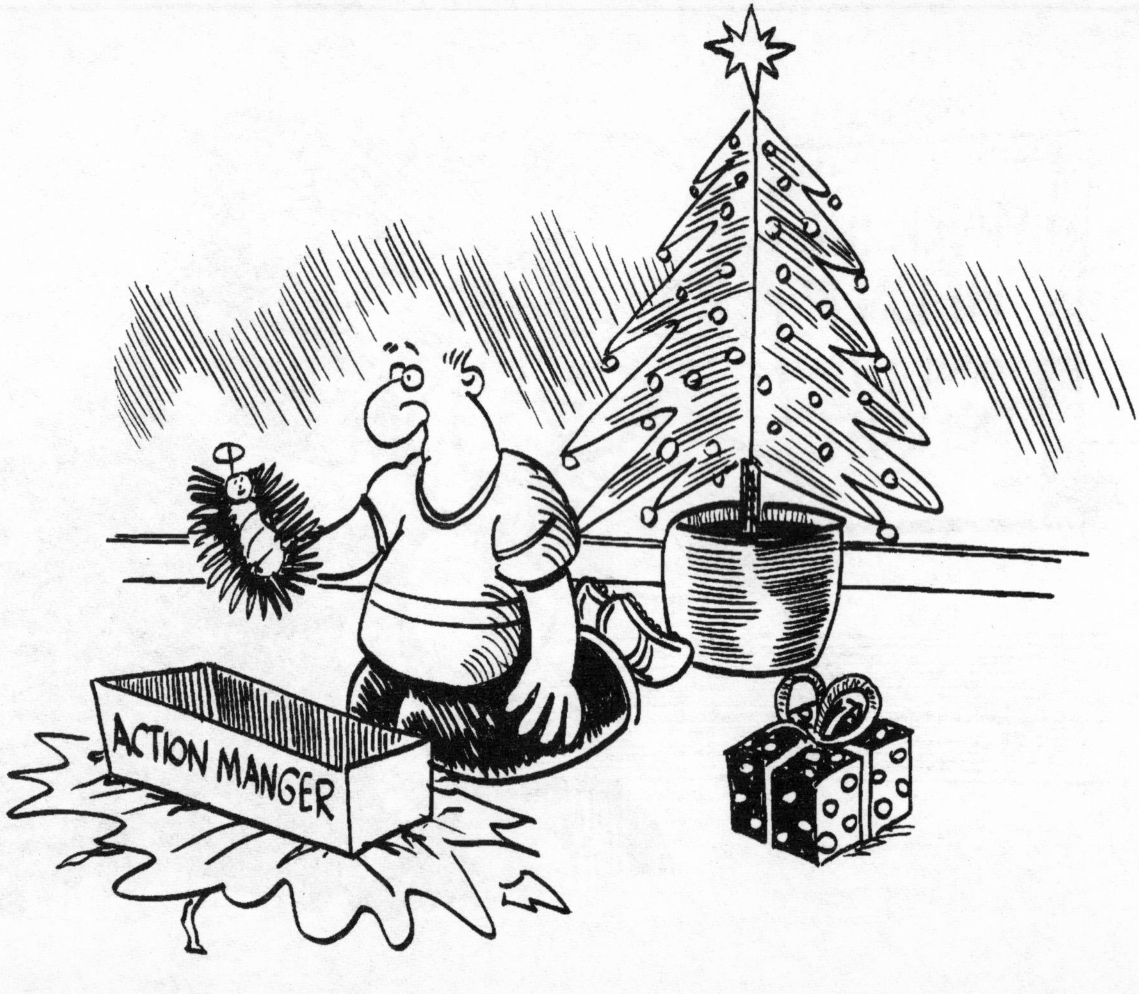
ACTION MANGER

greeting card empire. Hallmarcus went on to develop Mother's Day, Father's Day and Valentine's Day, as well as the less successful Gladiator's Day and Centurion's Day. His 'Good luck in the Colosseum' cards were particularly popular among the Christians at the time.

The Christmas cracker

What kind of mind came up with the Christmas cracker? Two people battle for possession of a small useless plastic object and a hat made of paper in a contest based primarily on strength. If it didn't already exist, it seems likely that Channel 4 would eventually have got around to developing the game show.

The true origin of the Christmas cracker stretches back to biblical times when Christians found themselves on the menu at the Colosseum. In order to warm up the crowd before the real blood-letting began, two Christian children would fight for a toy weapon – usually a 3-inch sword – which was wrapped in muslin and set alight. The contest would involve much tugging and burning of flesh, after which the winner would receive a crown made of parchment.

In recent times, with the advent of social workers, the burning of children's flesh has become less acceptable and has been replaced by a small firecracker, although the useless contents and paper hat remain to this day. The appalling riddles and jokes are a modern phenomenon and are all written by Bob Monkhouse.

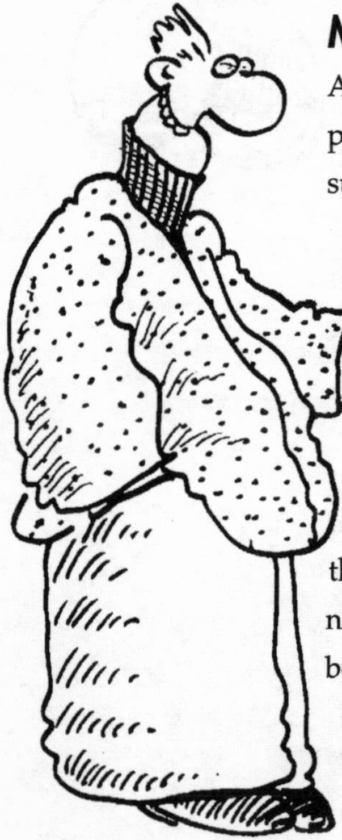

Mulled wine

As the name suggests, mulled wine is wine that has been contemplated and pondered at length, as observers try to figure out the reason for adding spices, sugar, cinnamon sticks and oranges to red wine before heating the strange concoction. Just how intoxicated was the creator of this bizarre recipe? Even Piat d'Or tastes better without a little sugar, nutmeg and a bus load of oranges thrown in, although it is true that many Bulgarian wines benefit from the addition of any extra ingredients, even sweat and disinfectant.

Intensive trawling of the Bible has failed to throw up any links between mulled wine and the birth and life of Christ and, indeed, there is documentary evidence that the wine miraculously produced at the wedding feast of Cana was definitely not mulled. In John 2:10 the steward tells the bridegroom that 'you have kept the best wine until now', rather than exclaiming, 'what sort of piss is this?'

The tradition most probably originated with some down-and-outs attempting to keep warm one Christmas Eve with a bottle of cheap plonk, some assorted spices and a Jaffa orange. These would be known as mulled winos.

Rough Guide to Bethlehem

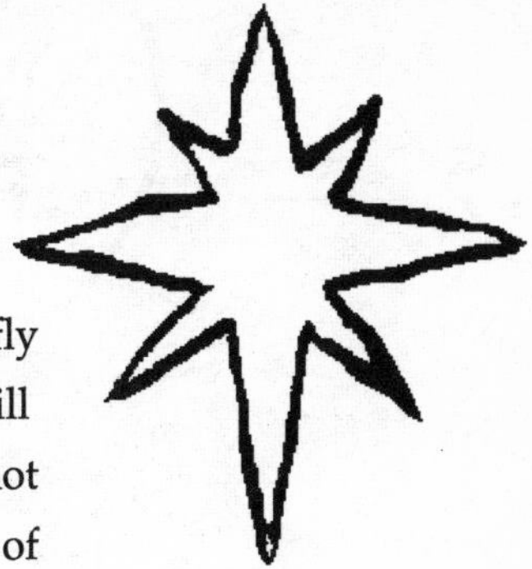

Getting there

Simply follow the bright light, making sure to keep one eye on the road. By air, fly into Nazareth and then take a donkey to Bethlehem. If travelling by ferry, you will first arrive in the port of the Dead Sea, which, as the name suggests, is not renowned for its night life. This quaint seaside town has an extensive range of funeral homes but no zombies, who tend to flock to the Undead Sea. Again, donkeys are available for hire to take you to your destination.

Red tape

None, but there is a Red Sea nearby.

Money

In this part of the world financial transactions take place in the temples. Daily masses are held in most post offices, while the banks offer confession as well as foreign exchange facilities.

Health

Bethlehem offers modern care with the added benefit of miracles, which can result

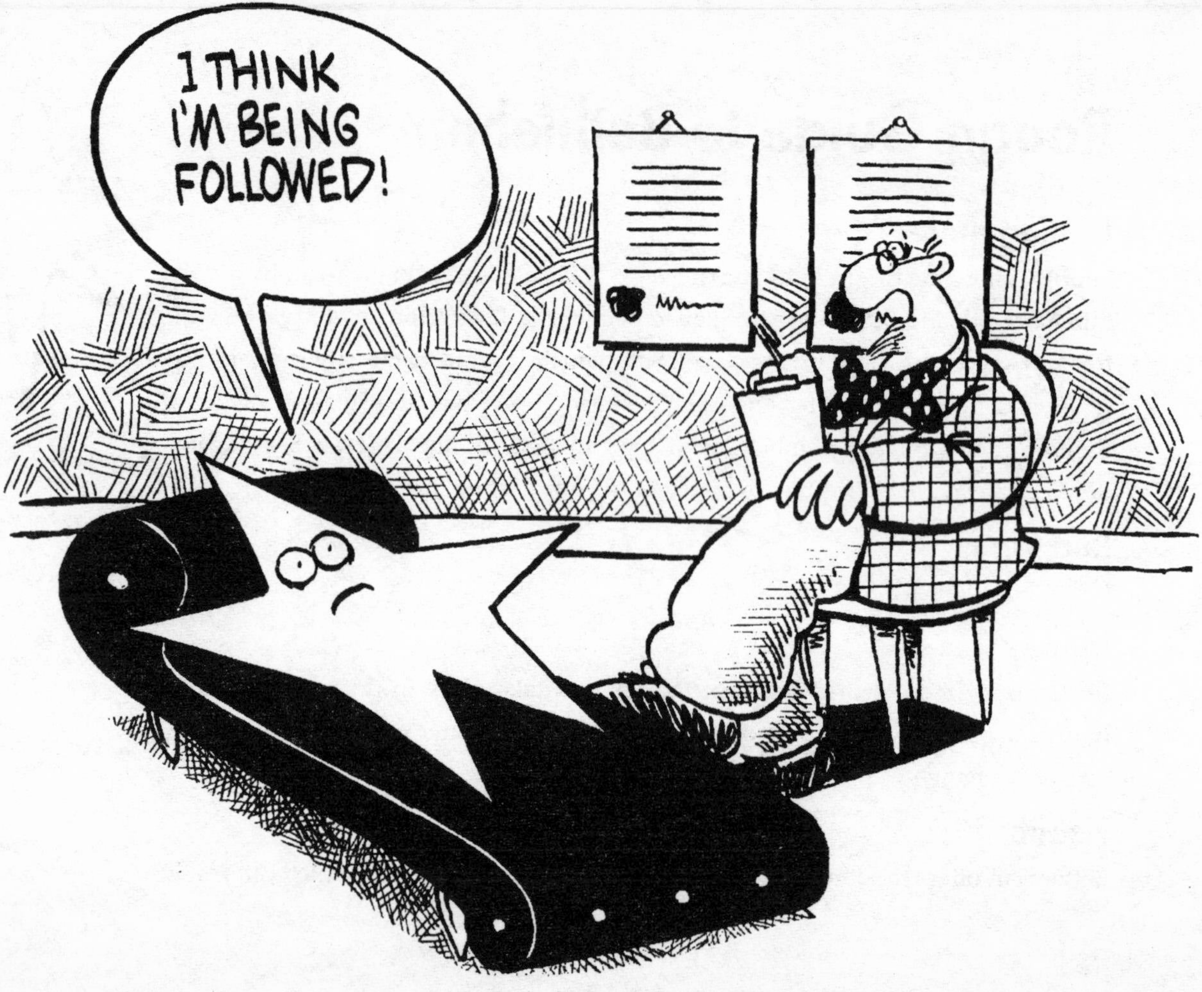
I THINK I'M BEING FOLLOWED!

in the lame walking and the dead rising. However, pregnant women are advised to avoid Bethlehem as birthing facilities are sparse.

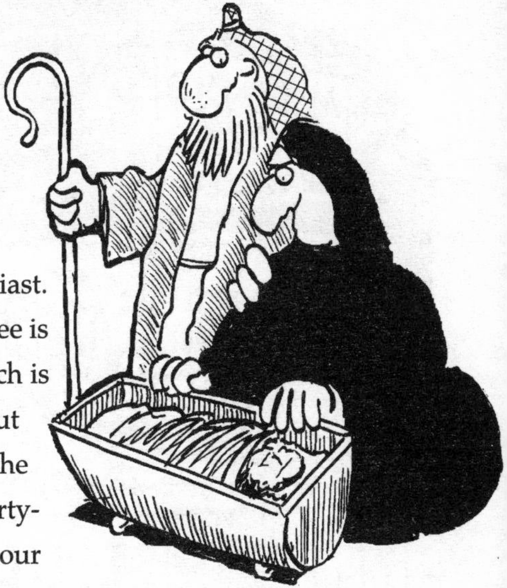

Insurance

As well as the usual travel insurance, it might be wise to take out a life policy on your first-born child.

Amenities

Regular day trips to the Dead Sea cater for the water sports enthusiast. For those who don't mind travelling that bit further, the Sea of Galilee is a wonderful amenity. Try skiing, boating, or walking on water, which is a speciality of this region. Fishermen are, of course, common here, but beware – they have a tendency to drop their nets and follow you at the slightest invitation. Much of the surrounding area is desert and forty-day field trips can be arranged for the curious. Remember to pack your own lunches and avoid temptation.

Accommodation

Bethlehem's night sky is renowned for its anomalies, making it a favourite destination for astronomical conferences, which tend to book up all the hotel space, leaving no room at the local inns for the casual tourist, particularly in December.

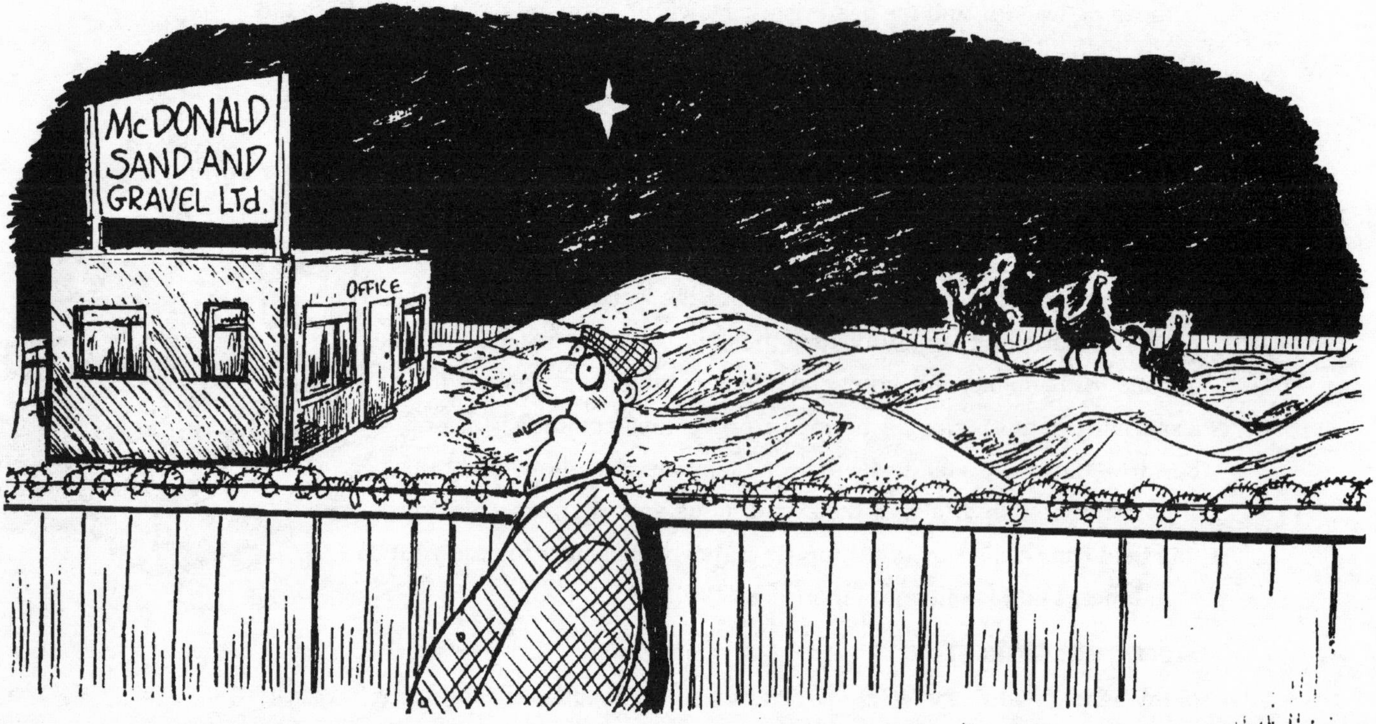
McDONALD
SAND AND
GRAVEL Ltd.
OFFICE

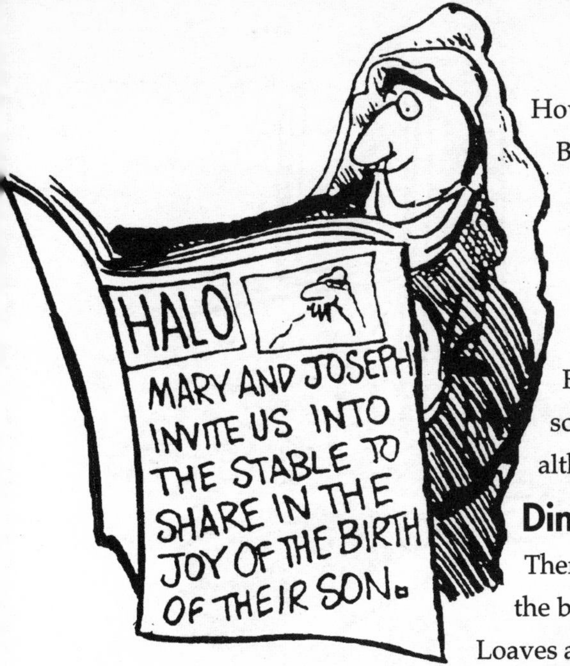
HALO
MARY AND JOSEPH INVITE US INTO THE STABLE TO SHARE IN THE JOY OF THE BIRTH OF THEIR SON.

However, if you're prepared to rough it a little, Bethlehem is famous for its selection of cosy if somewhat basic stables. Most are child-friendly and come with fitted baby manger.

What to buy

Bethlehem's biggest sellers include body oils such as Frankincense by Armani and Calvin Klein's popular scent Myrrh – both available in the local Body Shop, although it is cheaper to buy duty-free.

Dining out

There are plenty of restaurants in Bethlehem, although the biggest crowds are usually to be found at the famous Loaves and Fishes. This restaurant offers exceptional value and the whole family can dine for next to nothing. If you're looking for a quiet drink, try Herod's Place, but the more lively tourist would be advised to pay a visit to Cana – a wine bar where the vino, quite literally, flows like water.

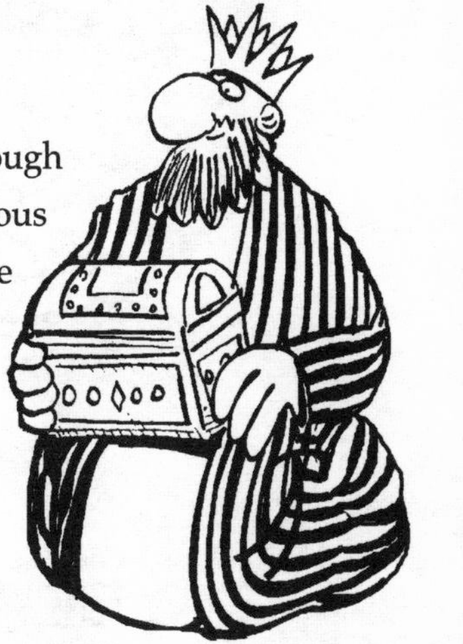

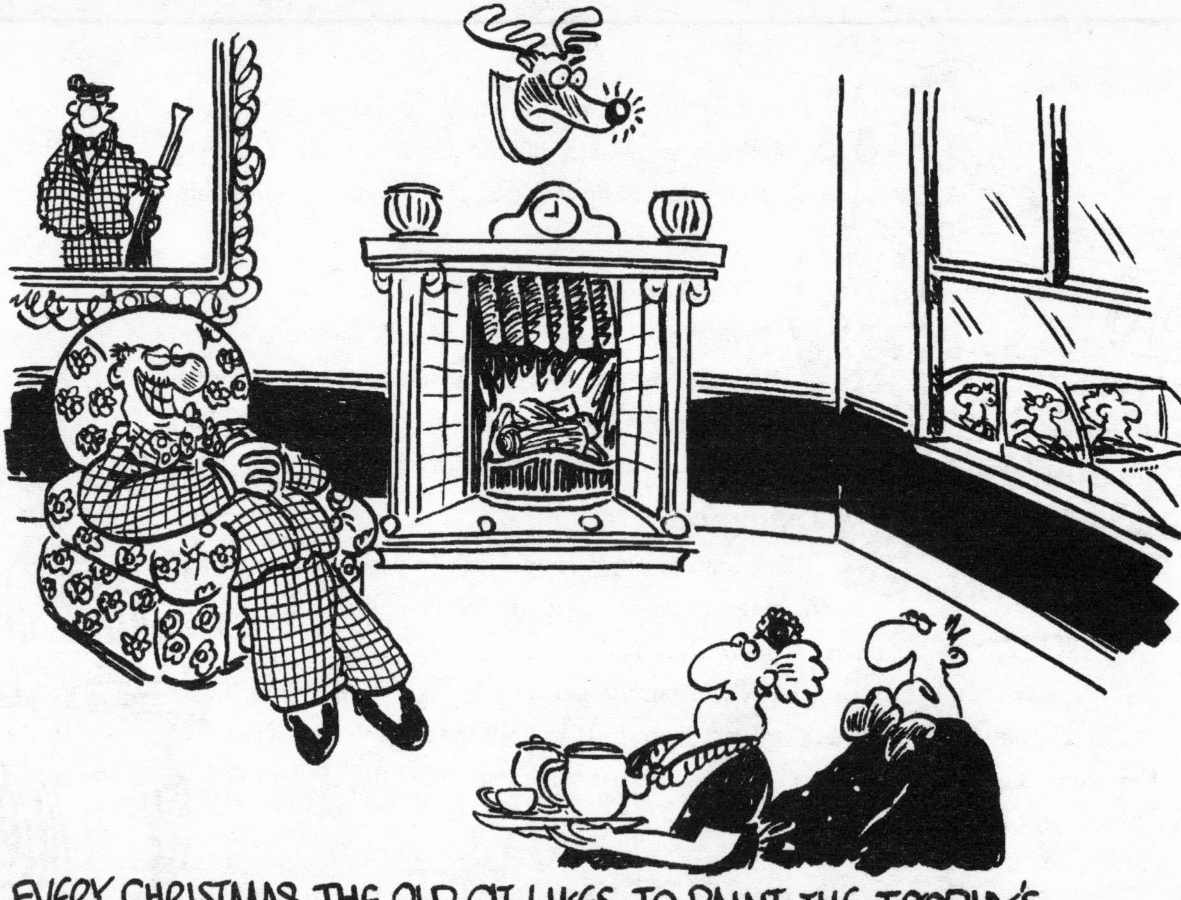

EVERY CHRISTMAS THE OLD GIT LIKES TO PAINT THE TROPHY'S NOSE RED AND UPSET THE GRANDCHILDREN....

A Guide to Santa's Reindeer

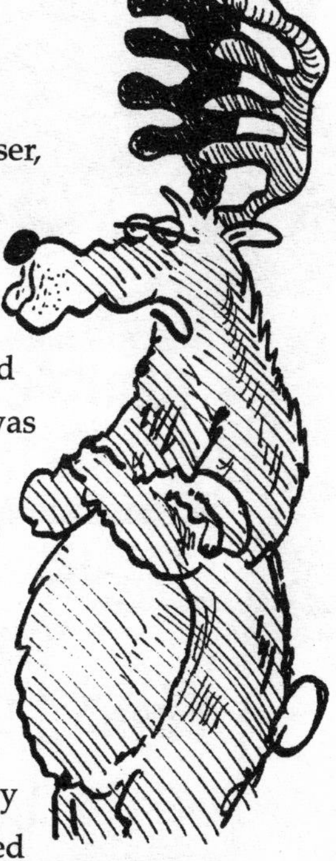

Who are they?

Rudolph, Prancer, Riverdancer, Hale-Bopp, Nike, Honda, Persona, Budweiser, Baywatch.

History

As every good child knows, there were originally eight reindeer who guided Santa's sleigh by night and while they did a pretty good job, their record was patchy and resulted in Santa recruiting a star name to lead from the front. Although the last to arrive, Rudolph the red-nosed reindeer has, today, the highest profile of Santa's reindeer, which, not surprisingly perhaps, leads to a lot of disharmony and jealousy among the rest of the crew, who consider him Santa's pet.

Santa has always denied any favouritism, however, and claims that the eight original reindeer were simply not pulling their weight and were grounded by poor weather conditions far too often. His decision to upgrade was, he says, 'based on market expectations' and a need to remain competitive. Although the workers

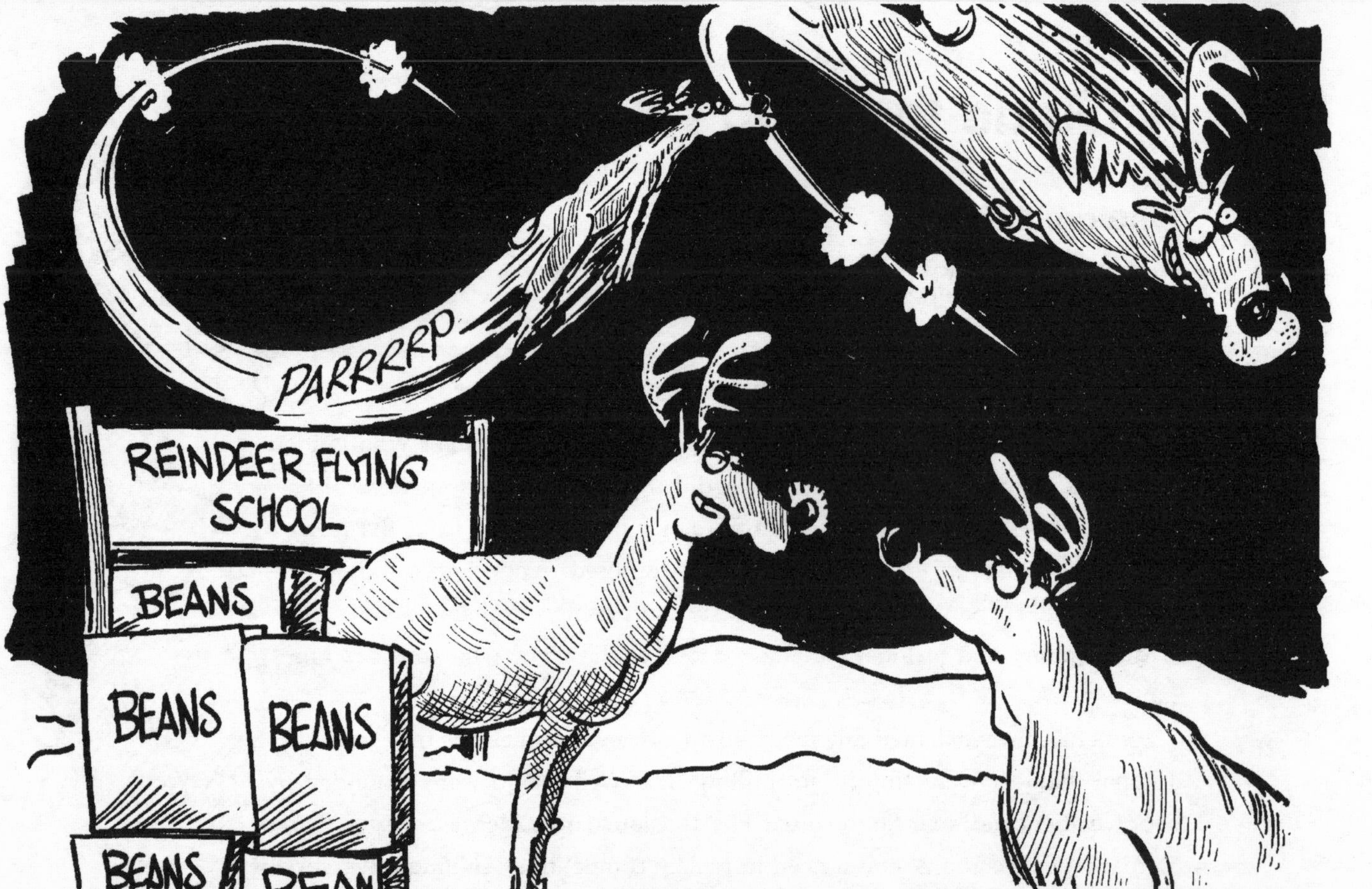
PARRRRP
REINDEER FLYING SCHOOL
BEANS
BEANS
BEANS
BEANS

WELL HOW THE HELL DO YOU THINK WE FLY... WE'RE REINDEERS!

initially desisted, Rudolph was finally accepted as part of an overall restructuring package, which saw the introduction of extra mileage allowance and improved bedding conditions.

What do they eat?

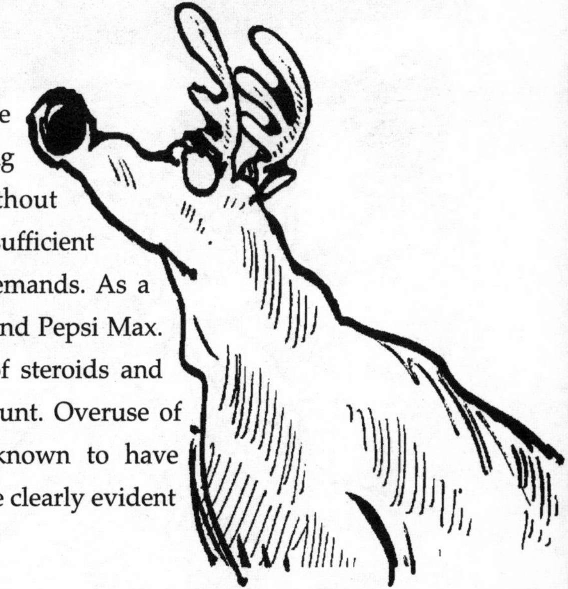

The diet of the reindeer is highly specialised, as they are asked to become airborne and carry a weight exceeding 450,000 tonnes at high speed over vast distances without refuelling of any kind. Normal diets do not provide a sufficient energy-per-kilo ratio to facilitate such massive physical demands. As a result, Santa's reindeer diet is high in Mars Bars, Snickers and Pepsi Max. In December the diet is supplemented with huge doses of steroids and blood-doping to significantly increase the haemoglobin count. Overuse of these drugs is considered dangerous and Rudolph is known to have developed a steroid dependency, the side effects of which are clearly evident at night.

How can they fly?

Although reindeer don't have wings or rotors, they do have aerodynamic ears

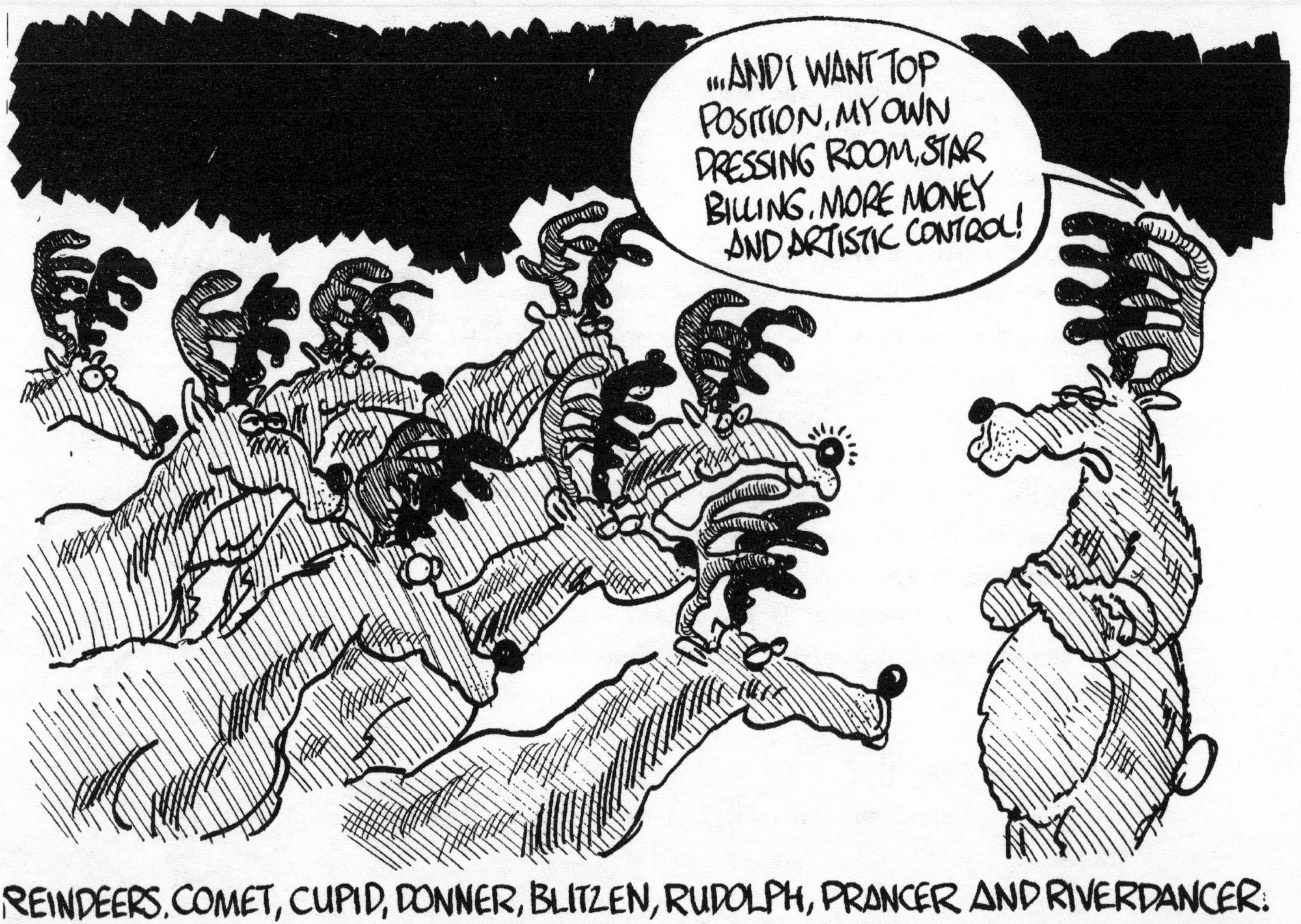
...AND I WANT TOP POSITION, MY OWN DRESSING ROOM, STAR BILLING, MORE MONEY AND ARTISTIC CONTROL!

REINDEERS. COMET, CUPID, DONNER, BLITZEN, RUDOLPH, PRANCER AND RIVERDANCER.

which ensure minimal wind resistance at high speed. The flight capability is based on a cross between the flying squirrel and the space shuttle, involving massive blast-off of approximately 12 billion kilos per square centimetre combined with the ability to leap from tree to tree with great grace. They do, of course, spend approximately eleven months a year in intensive training at subzero temperatures, although test flights are rare because of the huge physical demands and the possibility of airborne collision.

What about the sleigh?

Based on the same light weight technology responsible for the Stealth Bomber, Santa's sleigh can travel at high speeds and is invisible to normal radar (hence the danger of collision if airborne outside its allotted Christmas Eve slot). It is a rather large sleigh which must be capable of carrying enough toys for every good Christian child on the planet. While Santa's elves are the most efficient packers in the world, the 1–2 million tonnes of merchandise still require a sleigh approximately the size of an average cruise liner, which explains the need for steroids.

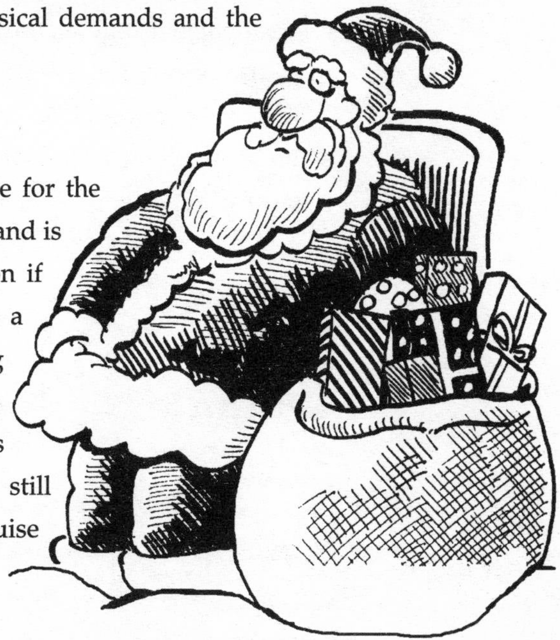

Will Rudolph go down in history?

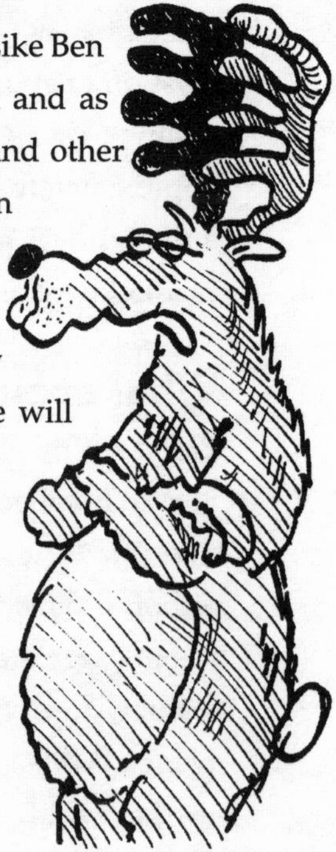

This seems highly likely, as the words of the popular song suggest. Like Ben Johnson, Rudolph's steroid abuse is certain to catch up with him and as leader of the team, an eventual collision involving Santa's sleigh and other aircraft cannot be ruled out. Such a disaster would not only result in disappointed children on a global level, but the devastation caused by the massive sleigh hurtling to the ground at speeds approaching that of light would be considerable. If Rudolph does eventually break down over a major conurbation, the subsequent loss of life will ensure that he will, indeed, go down in history.

No Entry

On his tour Santa Claus is not infallible and sometimes makes mistakes, startling unsuspecting non-Christians by the arrival in their house of a large bearded man with a sack. Even among Christians there are those who would rather be left alone, who find the annual visit more trouble than it's worth and who simply don't like Scandinavians.

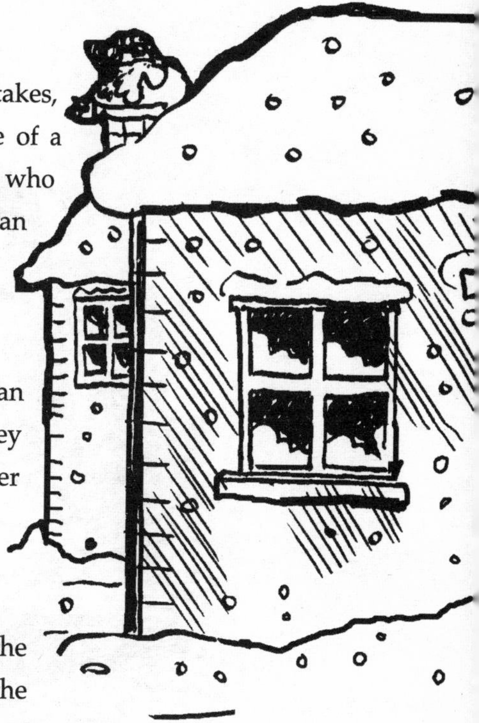

But can Santa be kept out?

Although cost-effective, chimney cowls do not provide much of an impediment to seasoned campaigners like Santa Claus, and while they may keep bird droppings out, burly Scandinavians are another matter altogether. If using a cowl, why not add some barbed wire or shards of glass? Santa, however, is determined and is unlikely to be dissuaded by such crude attempts.

A more effective strategy might be to add industrial lubricant to the roof, which prevents reindeer hooves gripping as they land. Due to the momentum of the massive sleigh and the huge speeds at which Santa

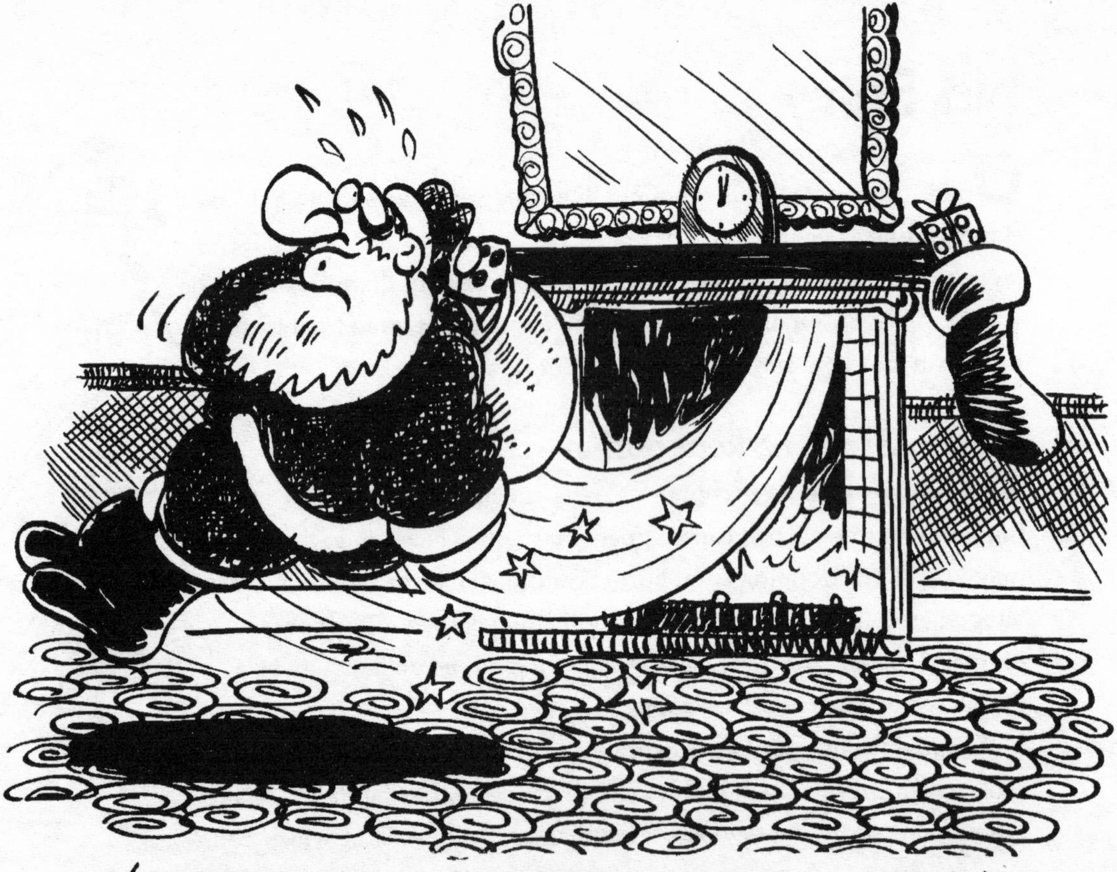

(WISHING YOU A VERY CRISP ARSE!)

travels, oil or grease can have quite an impact for little cost. But in the long term your roof could suffer from regular coatings with these products, resulting in an expensive reroofing job.

Reindeer traps are available and are particularly effective, if somewhat barbarous and costly. Take note that these traps have been condemned by both the Society for Prevention of Cruelty to Animals and Reindeer Rescue and are totally illegal. Furthermore, cat burglars have successfully sued for loss of limbs. In any case, Rudolph is now quite adept at spotting these traps, one of which almost sliced his nose off.

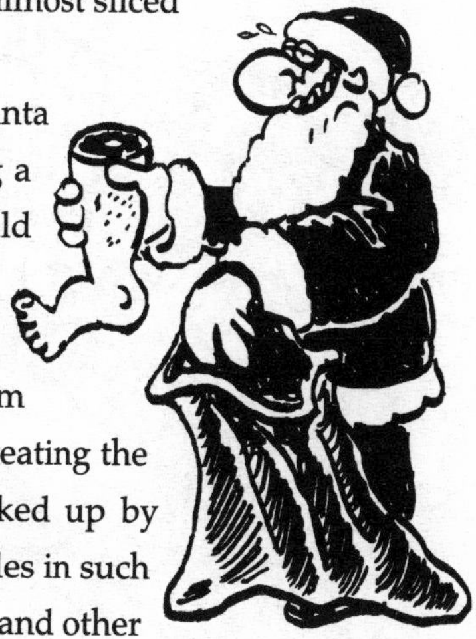

Scarecrows placed on the roof have proved partially effective but Santa Claus has developed sophisticated sensors to detect them, so chaining a real child to the roof is now the recommended option. While this should have the desired effect, it is well to remember that it is an offence under various laws of most countries in the Western world.

A simpler, and less objectionable, way to use children is to record them at play and then run the tape on Christmas Eve when you go to bed, creating the impression of activity below. These sounds will immediately be picked up by Santa on the roof, but in recent years he has taken to using stun grenades in such circumstances. Although mostly harmless, these can damage your hi-fi and other

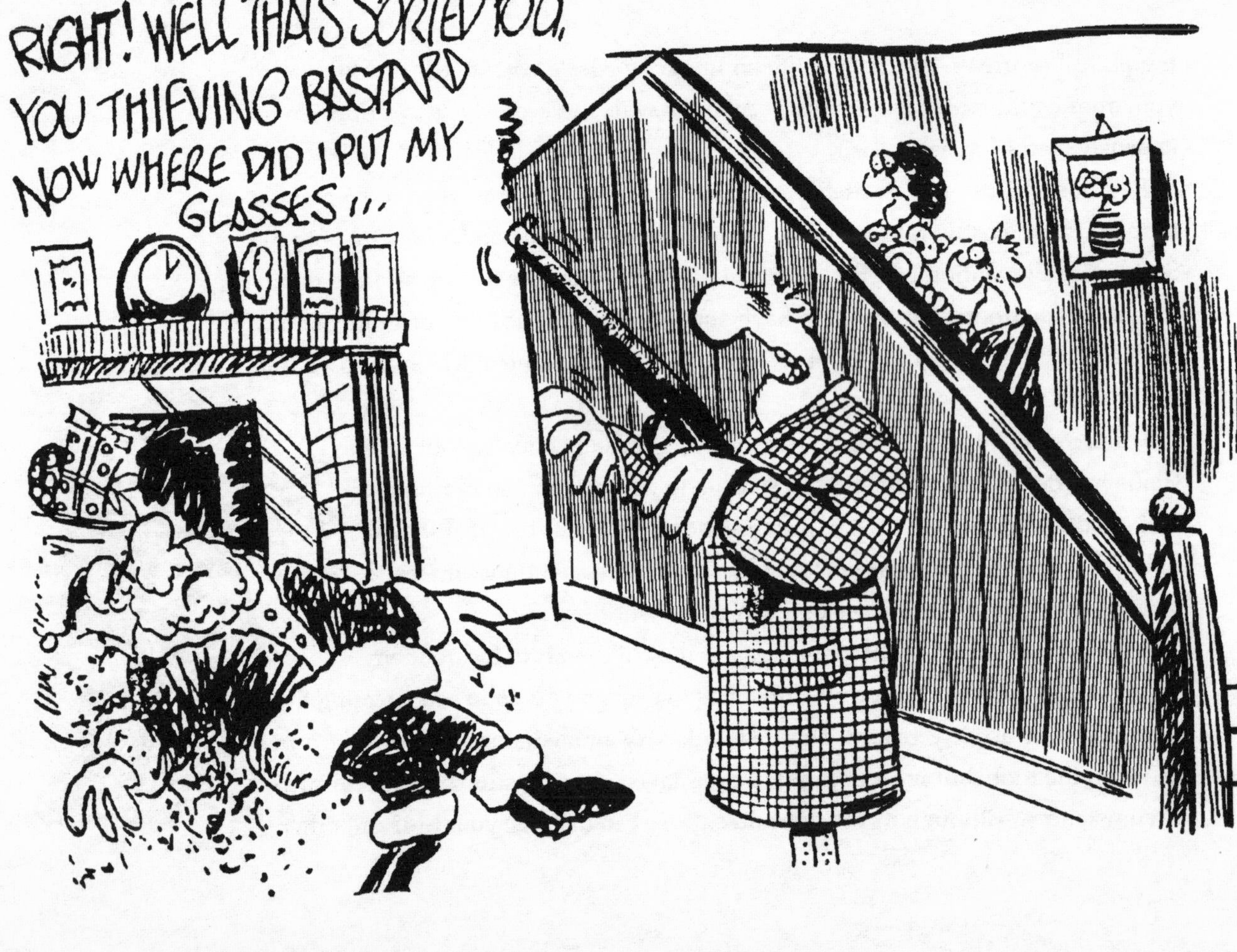
RIGHT! WELL THAT'S SORTED YOU,
YOU THIEVING BASTARD
NOW WHERE DID I PUT MY
GLASSES...

electrical devices in the room.

A dummy-chimney is a good lure away from the vulnerable entry points but is an expensive deterrent and requires planning permission. In the past most councils have proved reluctant to encourage such development because of the effect on low-flying aircraft and the dreams of young children.

So why not simply block up the fireplace? Blocking Santa's entry in this way will deprive you of the comfort of a real fire and merely encourage him to try other means of entry, such as French windows, coal chutes, skylights, etc. In fact, contrary to popular opinion, these are Santa's preferred modes of entry and the chimney today is rarely used, except in marketing and promotional material.

The fact of the matter is, an intruder as determined as Santa Claus is almost impossible to keep out without taking measures which break the law. However, it is believed that he is wary of legal action and a warning letter drafted by your solicitor and put up the chimney in mid-November would ensure that Santa is made fully aware of the threat of litigation should he be caught trespassing on your property. Although the High Court does not actually recognise Santa's existence, this is unlikely to prevent a lengthy and costly hearing taking place to determine the *locus standi* of Father Christmas, and the threat of such action may just be enough to deter him on Christmas Eve.

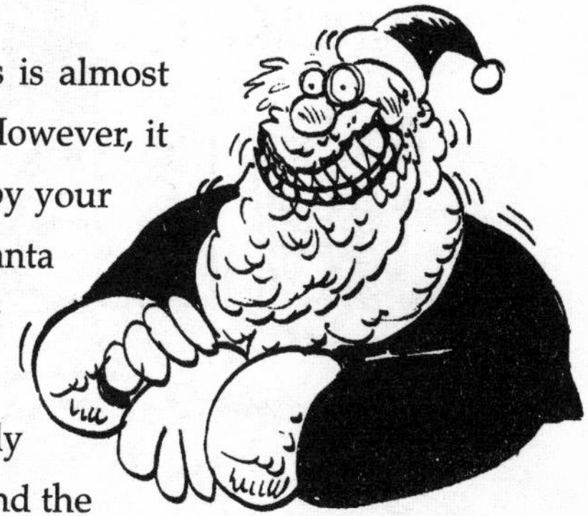

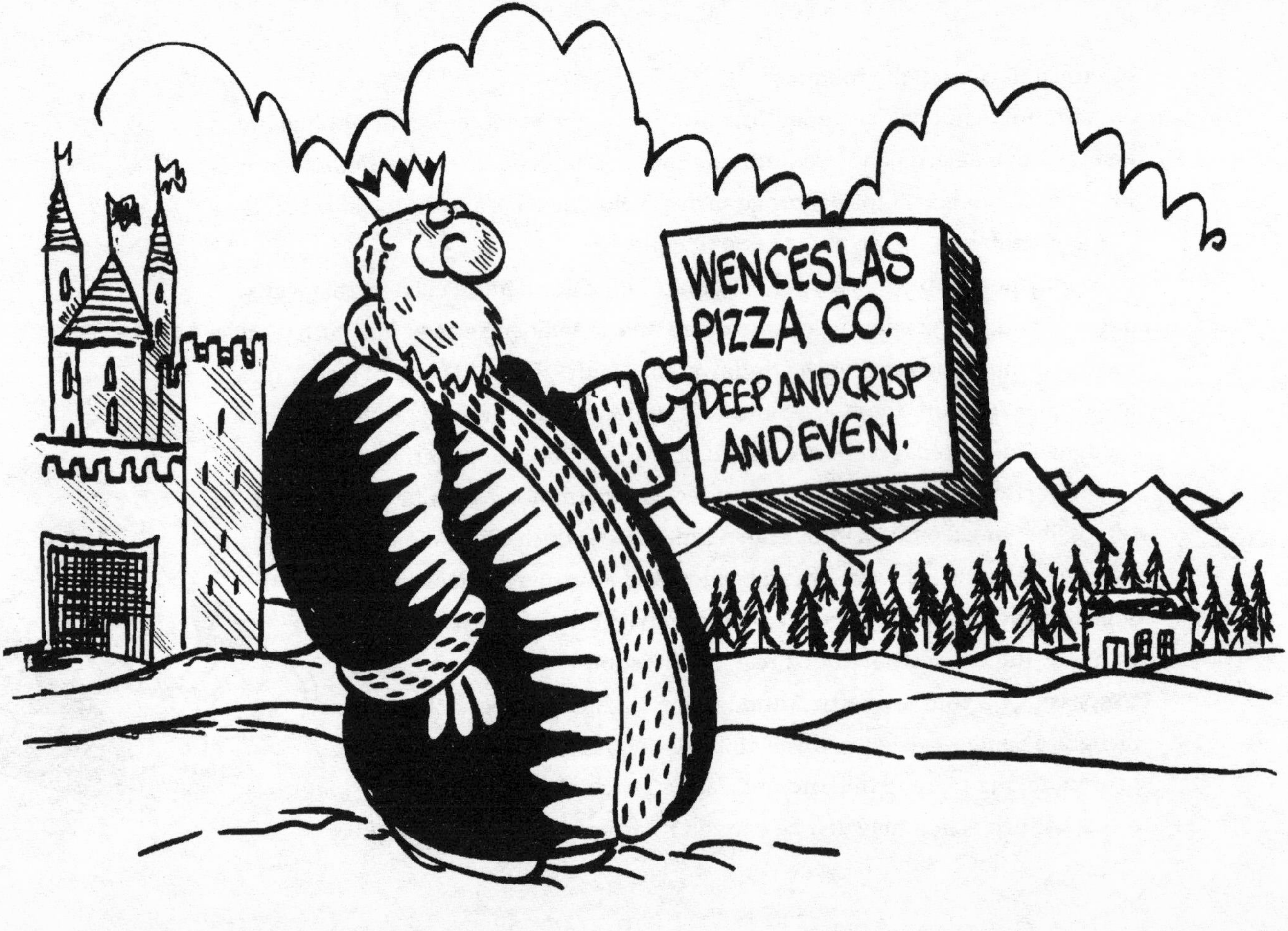
WENCESLAS
PIZZA CO.
DEEP AND CRISP
AND EVEN.

Who was
Good King Wenceslas?

One of the most familiar names associated with Christmas is that of Good King Wenceslas, but very little is known about this enigmatic Bohemian monarch.

To understand Good King Wenceslas (GKW), it is also necessary to know a little about Bad King Wenceslas (BKW) and Average King Wenceslas (AKW). This pair were GKW's predecessors on the throne of Bohemia during the fourteenth and fifteenth centuries, but their reigns were unimpressive. AKW was an ineffectual man whose policies had little impact on the public at large, although he did invest heavily in a military programme, which eventually led, some centuries later, to the development of a rifle named after him – the AK 47. Apart from this, however, AKW is completely forgotten. His successor BKW was, if anything, worse, and the people of Bohemia had little reason to be cheerful during his reign, which was notorious for his decision to put VAT on winter fuel. He died mysteriously in a blaze thought to have been started by a malicious subject known only as the BK Flamer.

GKW took over an unstable country, where, at night, poor men often came into sight gathering winter fuel – when the snow lay round about, deep and crisp and

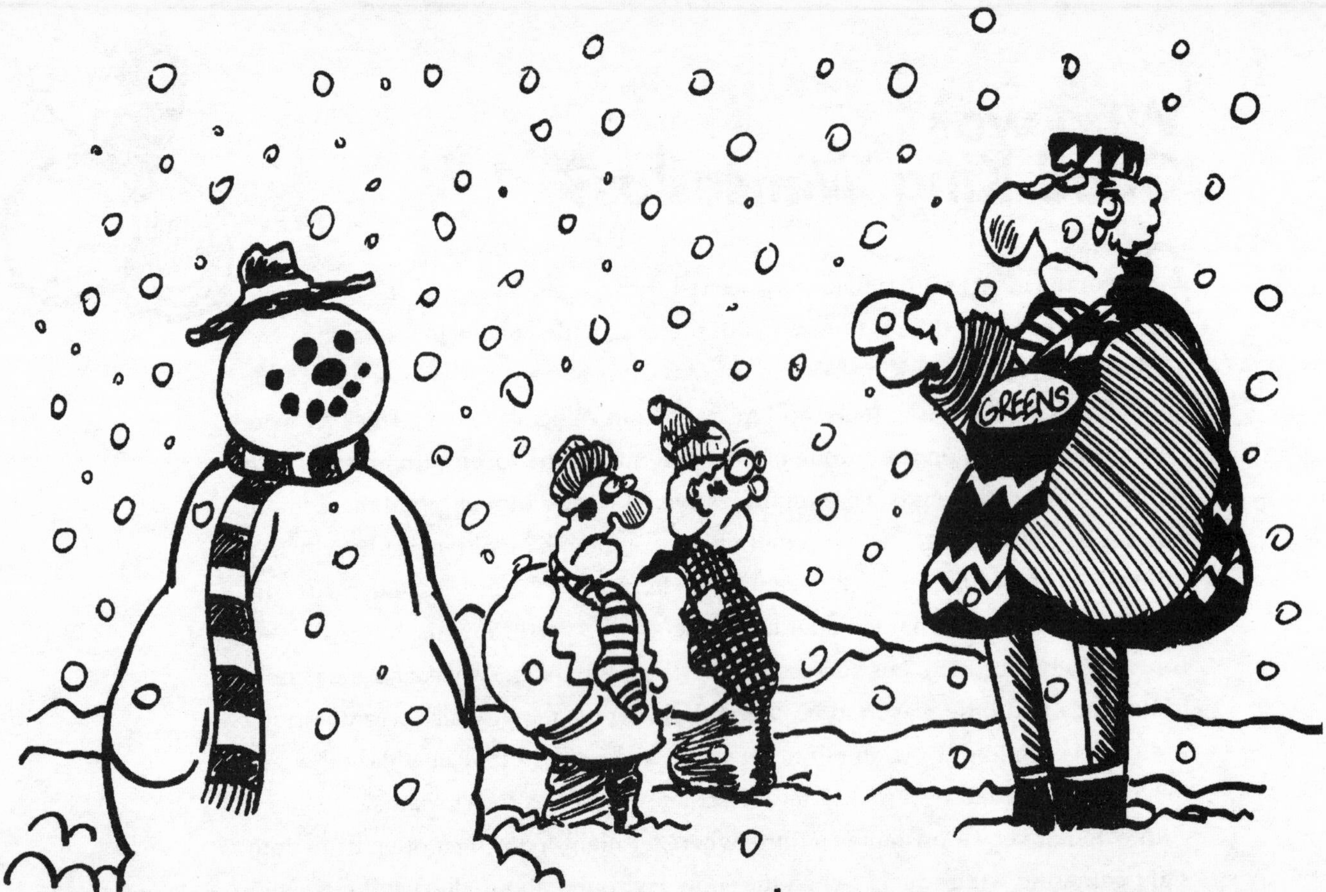
GREENS

AND I HOPE THAT'S SMOKELESS COAL YOU'RE USING YOUNG MAN...

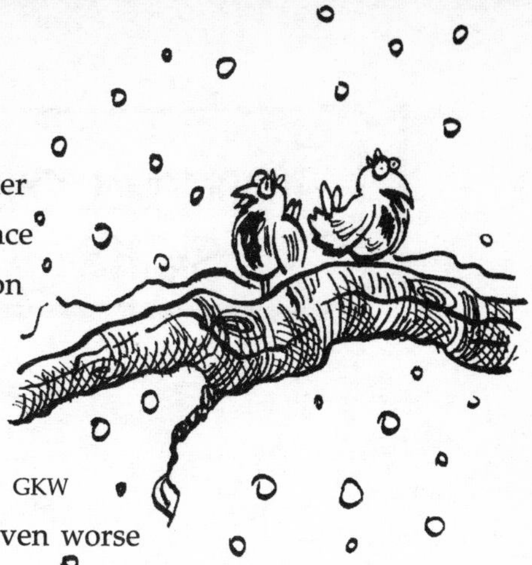

even. So desperate were they for warmth, that the people would gather their sticks even when the frost was cruel. It is said that GKW once witnessed such an act while sipping champagne on his balcony on Boxing Day and decided there and then to remove VAT from winter fuel. He also started a tradition of visiting the poor and bringing them wine and pine logs every feast of Stephen.

However, so cold was the weather in Bohemia at the time that GKW eventually caught pneumonia and died, leaving the country in an even worse mess than before, thanks to the growth of what was the first dependency culture in Europe. The social welfare bill had sky-rocketed during his reign, while his supporters were split on the notion of a welfare state and the then fledgling concept of a single European currency – leading to internecine feuding for years to come.

Stability was only restored after the arrival of NKW – New King Wenceslas – a young leader with vision and a top quality adviser, Evil King Mandelson. But NKW made many promises that were, of course, not kept, and he was soon forgotten.

It is Good King Wenceslas that we remember today, for his charitable acts in the snow and a hugely popular song, written in his honour by a poor man who, unfortunately, failed to secure the lucrative copyright for himself. But that is another story . . .

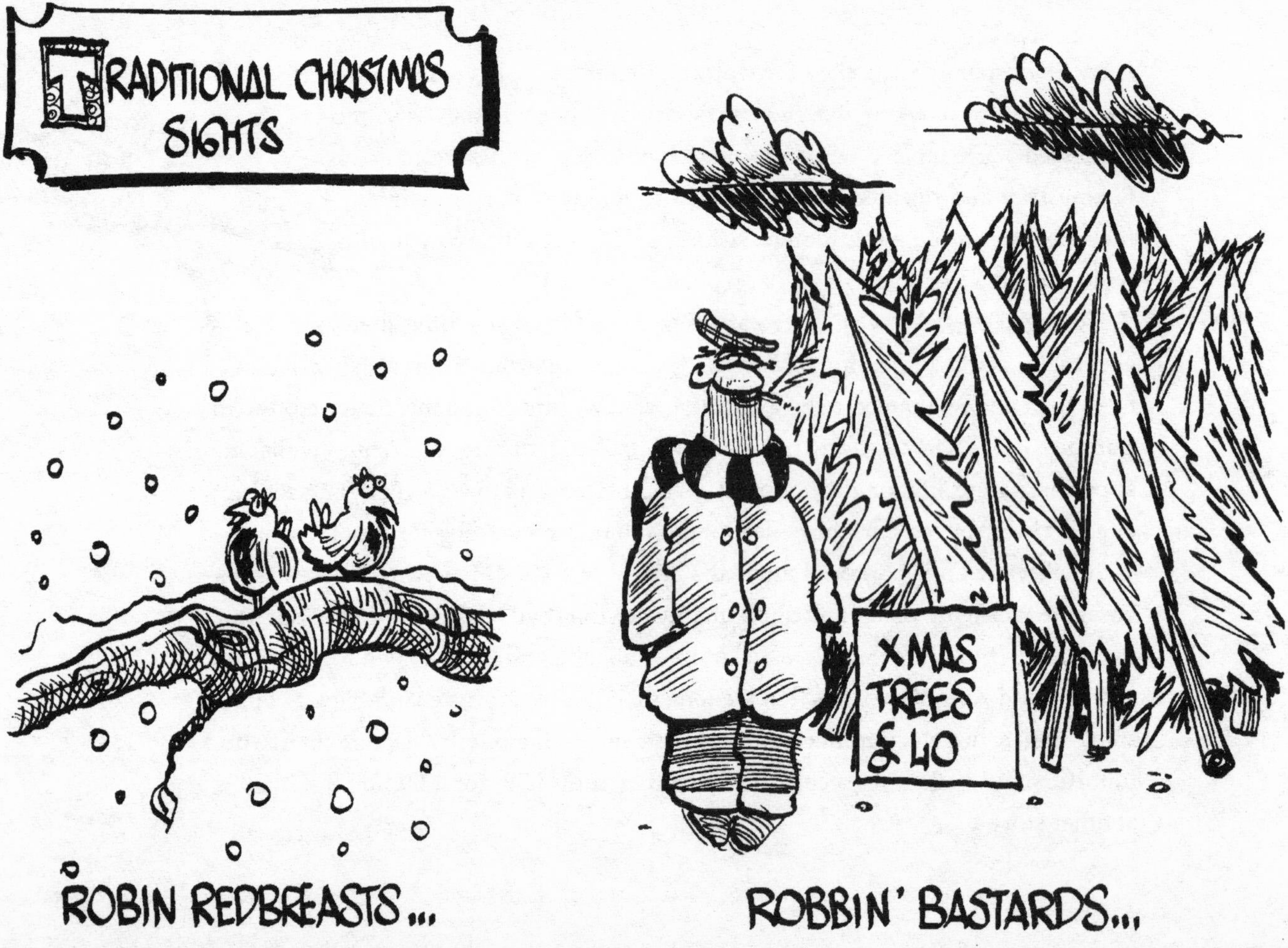
TRADITIONAL CHRISTMAS SIGHTS
XMAS TREES £40
ROBIN REDBREASTS...
ROBBIN' BASTARDS...

The Christmas Tree — How to Spot it

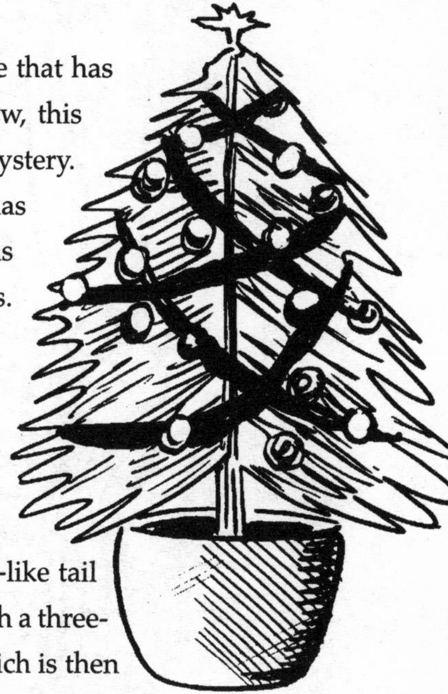

The Christmas tree – *Phylum Coniferous Yuletide* – is a wonder of nature that has intrigued botanists for generations. From an evolutionary point of view, this humble conifer has posed many questions and, even today, it is still a mystery.

Originating in Norway, the earliest scientific accounts of the Christmas tree (ref: the Bible – New Testament) suggest that today's specimen has developed a number of features that are exclusive to this species. Pyramidal in shape with needle-like leaves and light brown wood, the most striking difference is probably the multi-coloured flashing lights which cluster around the main body of the tree. These are known as 'fairy lights' because, in ancient times, it was believed that the lights were the work of the devil's spawn.

The illuminations apparently derive their energy from a small thread-like tail or 'cable', which runs along the branches before entering the earth through a three-pronged nodule, the 'plug'. This ability to produce and store energy, which is then released as pockets of intensely colourful light, is unique to the Christmas tree.

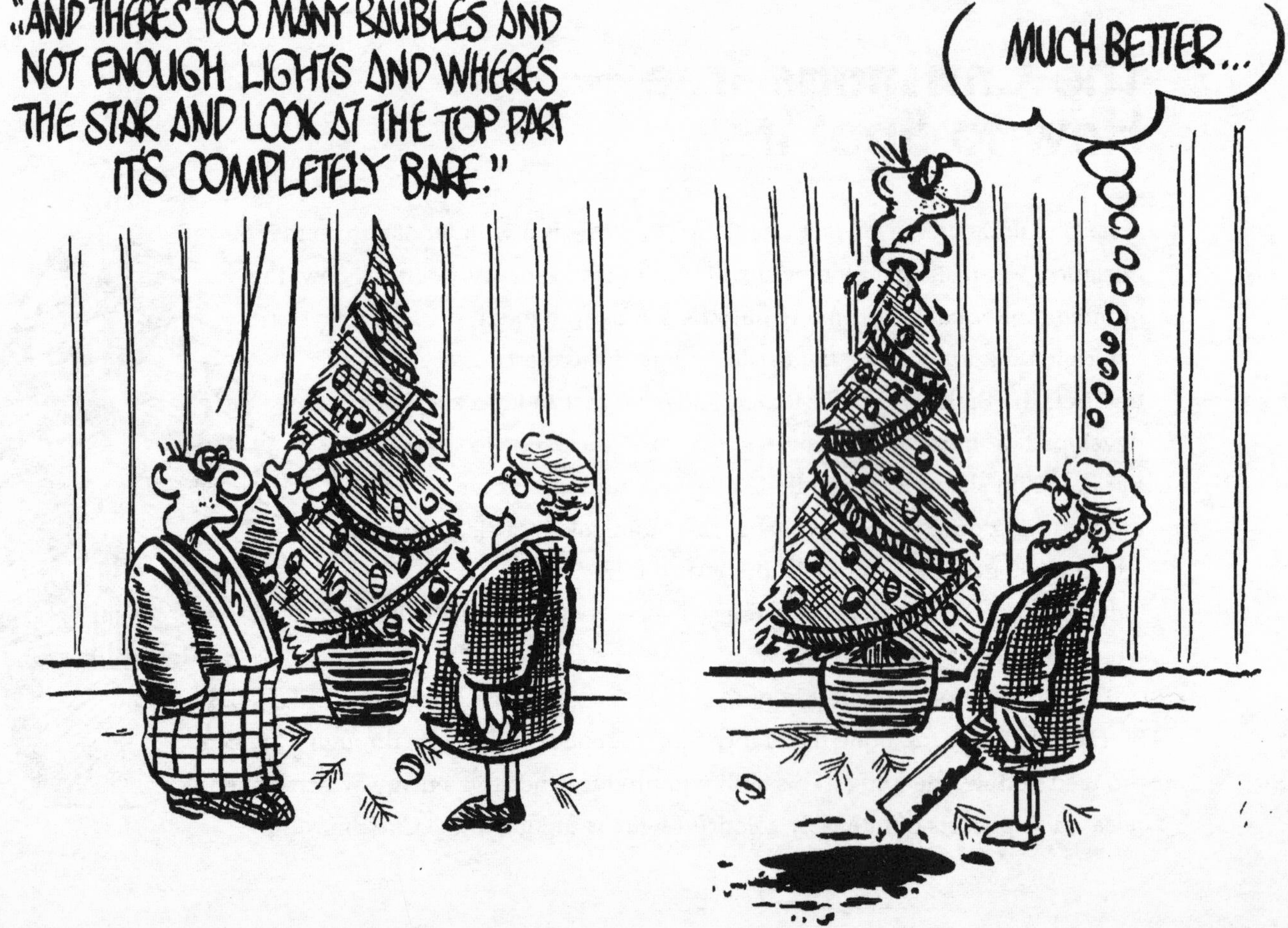
"..AND THERE'S TOO MANY BAUBLES AND NOT ENOUGH LIGHTS AND WHERE'S THE STAR AND LOOK AT THE TOP PART IT'S COMPLETELY BARE."
MUCH BETTER...

A second and equally perplexing feature of this species is the strange root system which has evolved into a sturdy base or 'stand', sometimes tripod in appearance, although this feature occurs in a variety of forms. This gives the tree stability, particularly on flat surfaces, while also rendering it taller. Along with the flashing lights, the presence of the 'stand' means that the student botanist will often be able to spot a Christmas tree even before graduation. However, it is not advisable to approach this species without being fully trained. This is because even the slightest contact can render the tree lopsided – a condition from which it rarely fully recovers.

A more recent evolutionary progression has been the blooming of a white structure at the apex of the tree. This is sometimes referred to as the 'angel', although some species have a star-like growth at this location. This trait is again unique to the Christmas tree, as is the effect – seen on some species – of 'false snow'. It is still far from clear how this stringy white substance is formed but it appears to act as a camouflage mechanism for the tree, probably scaring away potential parasites and household pets.

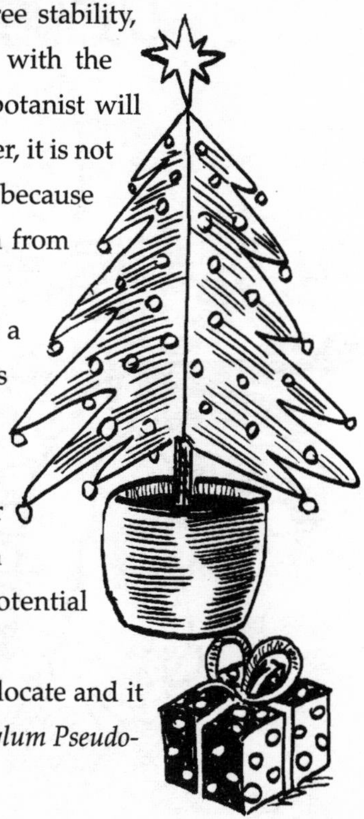

A word of warning to the curious. Christmas trees are not easy to locate and it is important to be on the lookout for a recent arrival in the forest – *Phylum Pseudo-*

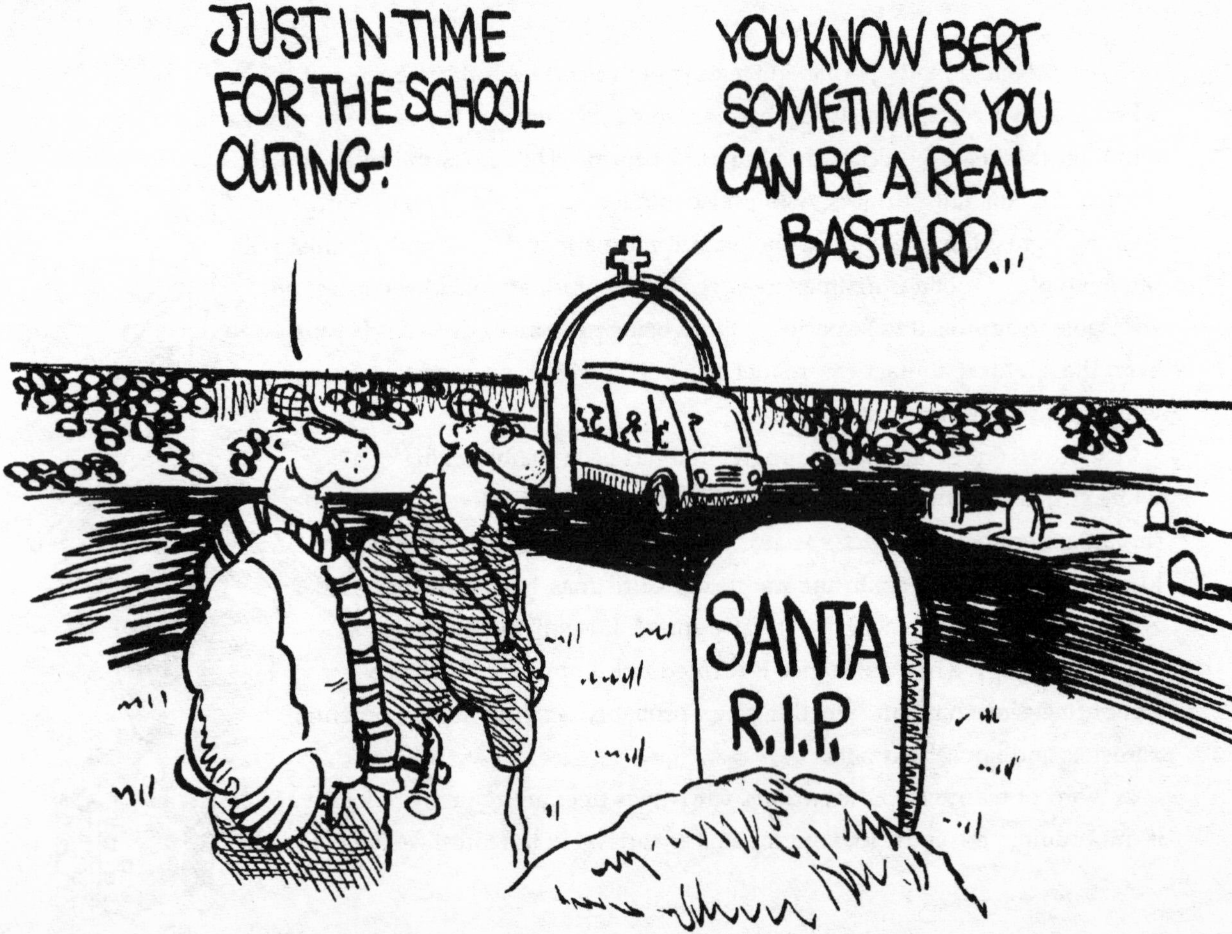
JUST IN TIME FOR THE SCHOOL OUTING!
YOU KNOW BERT SOMETIMES YOU CAN BE A REAL BASTARD...
SANTA R.I.P.

Coniferous Yuletide – the fake Christmas tree. This species has evolved many of the characteristics of the original, including the fairy lights, angel, stand and even fake fake snow. Some species have evolved yet further to include leaves of various lurid hues.

This species is far less popular than the *Phylum Coniferous Yuletide* but has proved a more sturdy tree, outliving its cousin by many years. Botanists believe that, in years to come, the pseudo variety may become the predominant species, although there are already groups protesting about the predominance of fake fir.

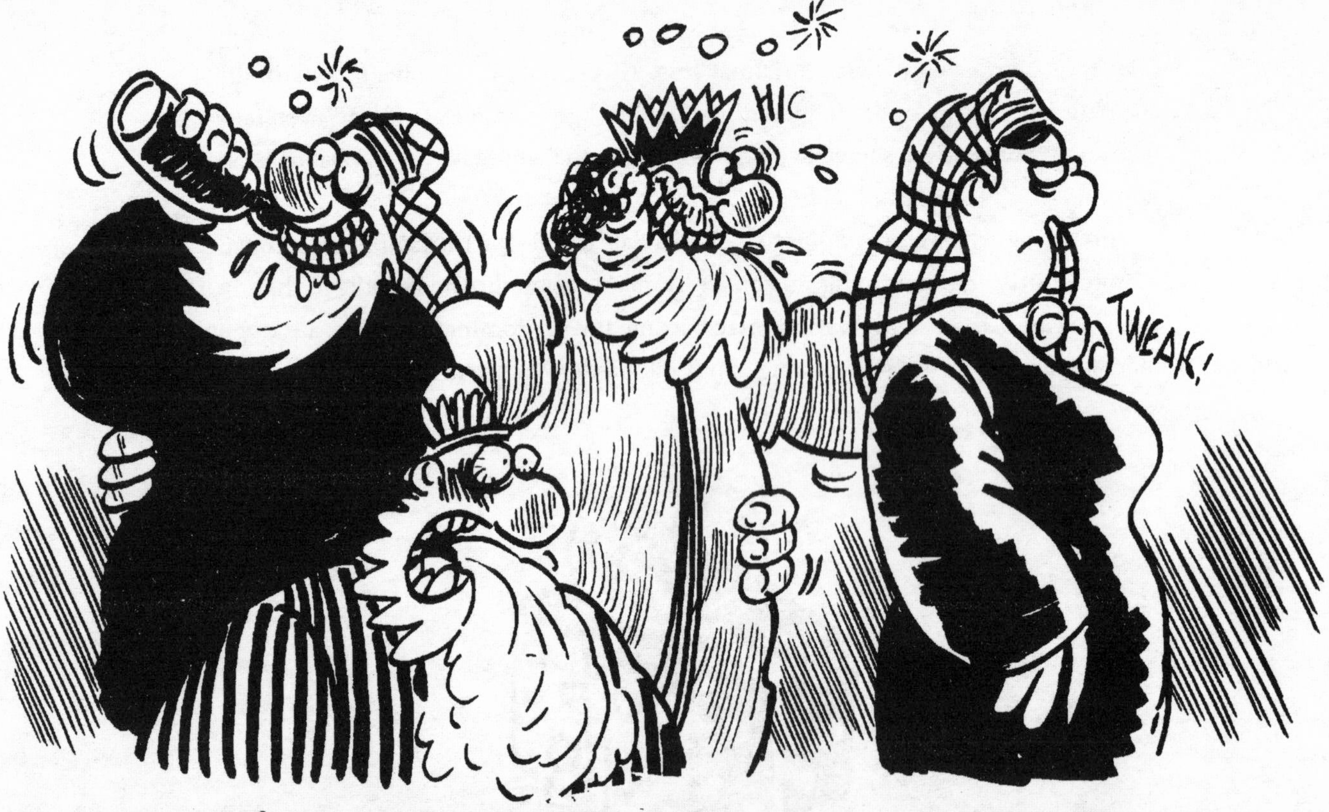
HIC
TWEAK!

(WISEMEN BEHAVING BADLY.)

The Family – How to Survive it on Christmas Day

Relative values

Christmas Day is full of surprises but, unfortunately, this doesn't include the relatives. They are nothing if not consistent, never failing to turn up and wreak havoc. Somehow the relatives have managed to become part of the tradition of Christmas, despite the obvious lack of appeal of such an invasion on such a day.

When did this aberration become a tradition, and how? Certainly the birth of Jesus was marked by a complete absence of aunts and uncles. There were three strange blokes from a distant land laden down with goodies, and a couple of unobtrusive shepherds. None of them caused a fuss and all left without having to be asked.

Today the wise men have been replaced by Auntie Mary, Uncle Jack and young Pat, and the gold, frankincense and myrrh have been replaced by talcum powder, socks and a selection box. And

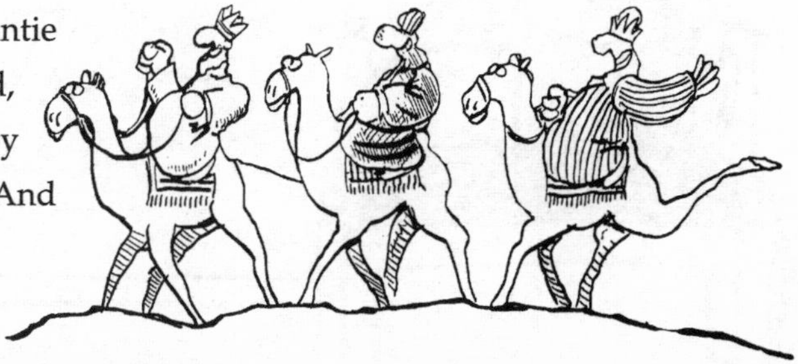

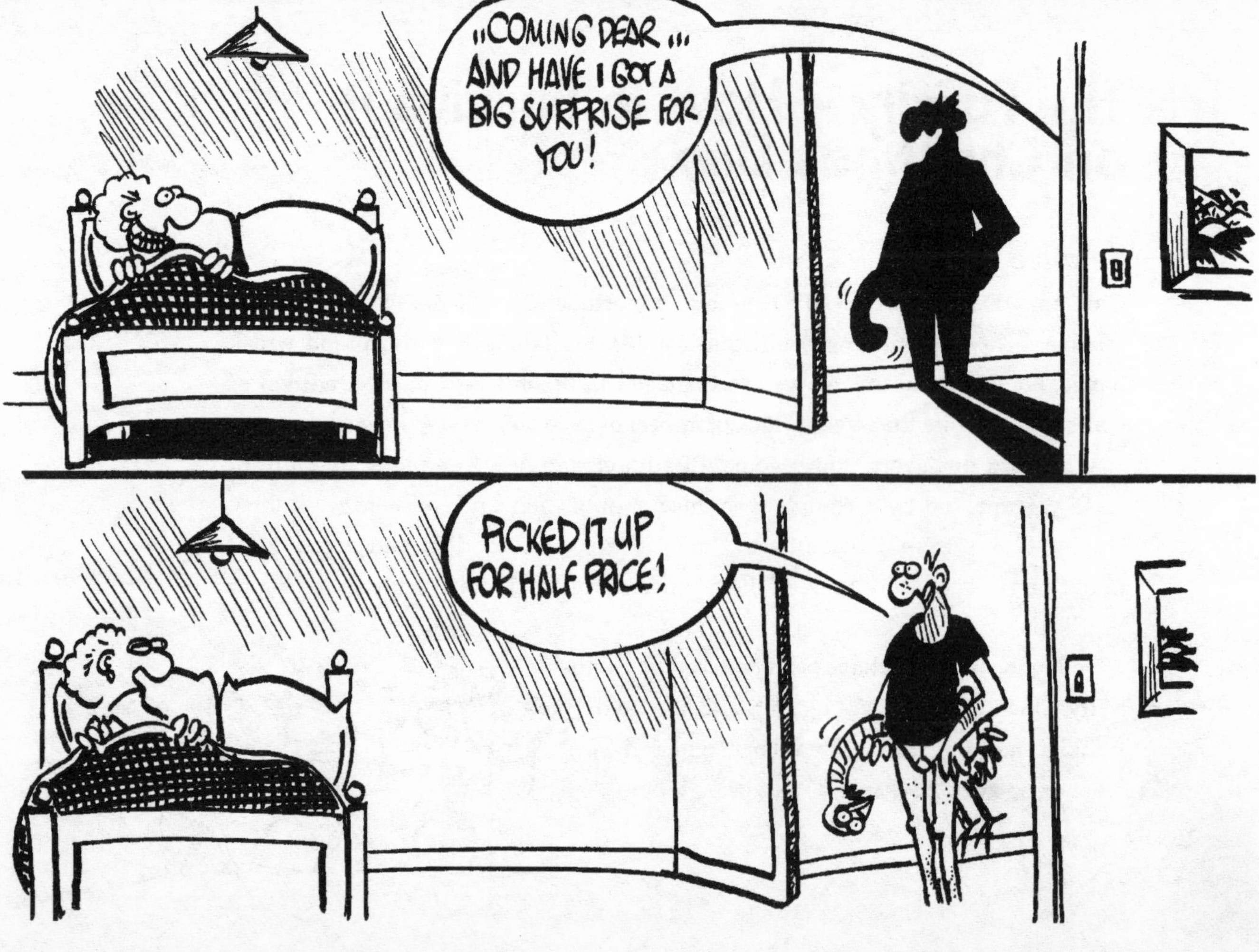
..COMING DEAR ... AND HAVE I GOT A BIG SURPRISE FOR YOU!
PICKED IT UP FOR HALF PRICE!

unlike the Magi, who are not thought to have invited themselves to dinner, the relatives don't tend to quietly disperse of their own accord. Getting rid of them can be like trying to . . . er . . . get rid of the relatives on Christmas Day.

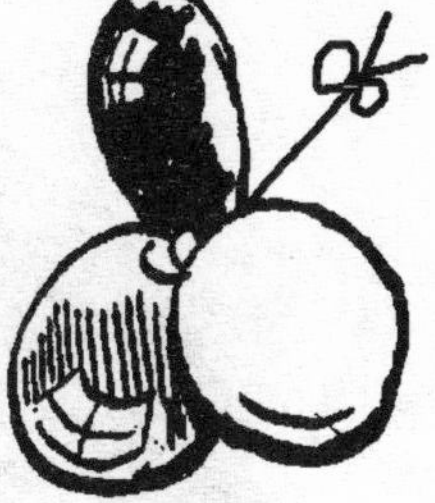

Ten ways to send the relatives packing

1 Announce an outbreak of Ebola virus in the dining room.
2 Discuss the recent installation of electric cabling overhead and the threat of bone marrow damage from the emitted radiation.
3 When the relatives are not looking, simply sneak out the back door and head for their house.
4 Stand to attention and play the national anthem.
5 Bring out the Ferrero Rocher.
6 Strip to your underwear and ask Auntie Mary to play strip poker.
7 Offer only diluted Babycham to the adults.
8 Offer only neat whiskey to the children.
9 Repeatedly ask to borrow money for a penile implant/breast enlargement operation.
10 Murder the relatives and dispose of the corpses. This is the most drastic, but always the most effective, option. However, it may also spoil Christmas somewhat for the younger members of the family.

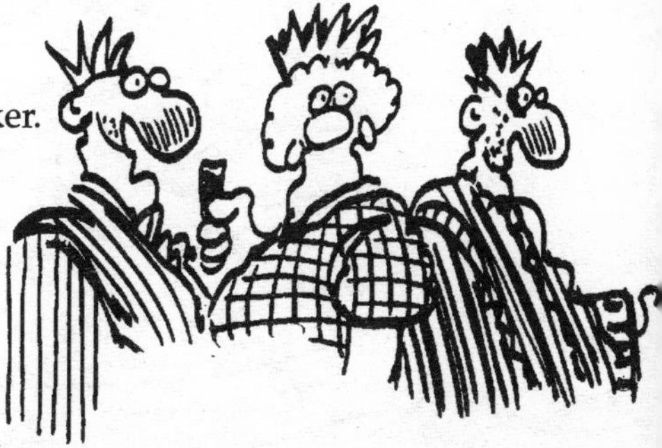

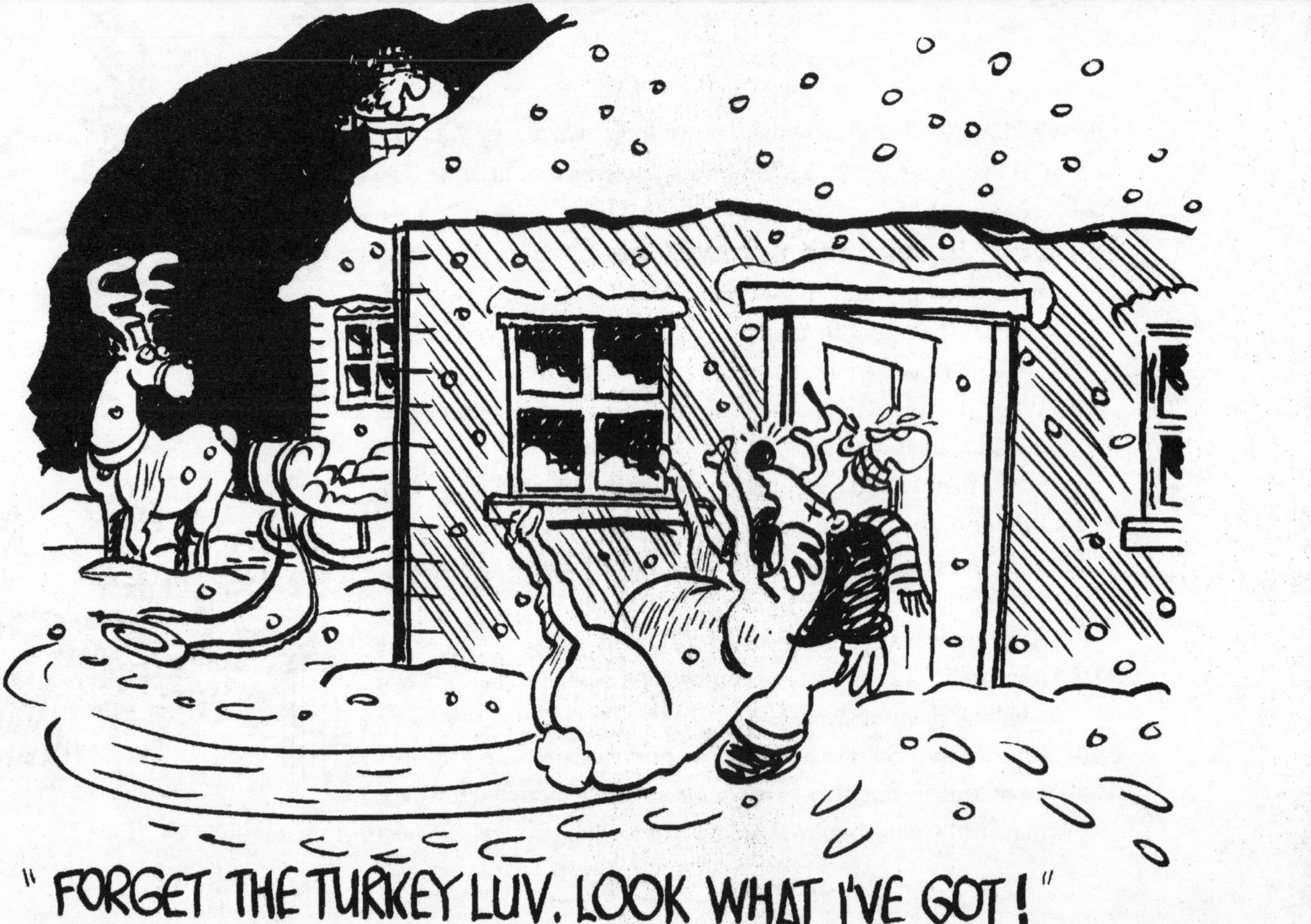

" FORGET THE TURKEY LUV. LOOK WHAT I'VE GOT ! "

Things to Avoid on Christmas Day

Christmas dinner

Christmas Day is not so much a celebration of the birth of Christ as the death of millions of turkeys. After Jesus was born in Bethlehem everyone felt a little peckish but the shepherds' sheep were considered too valuable and nobody wanted to slaughter any of the animals in the stable. However, when a turkey wandered by, one of the Magi leaped on it and slit its throat in a most impressive manoeuvre. So began a quaint Christmas tradition.

Turkey can be served in a variety of ways, all dead. It is a most unfortunate bird and, when introduced to America, where Christmas dinner is no big deal, the fowl instead found itself top of the menu for Thanksgiving Day – when 300 million Americans celebrate the genocide of the Native American people.

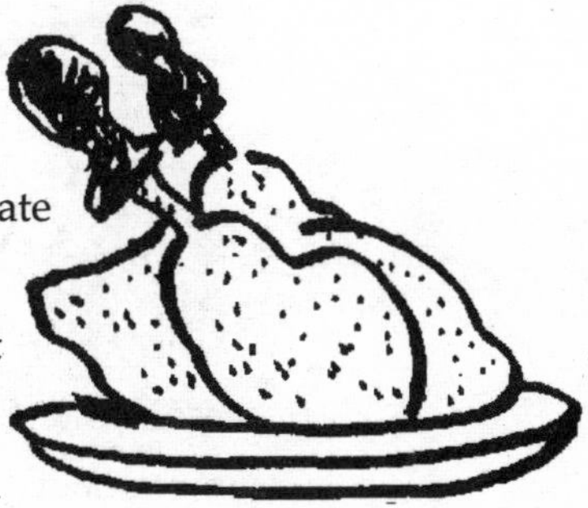

It was the Americans who added cranberry sauce to the dish, but as they eat peanut butter and jam, this is no surprise. What is a surprise is that the Europeans have adopted this bizarre mixture on Christmas Day.

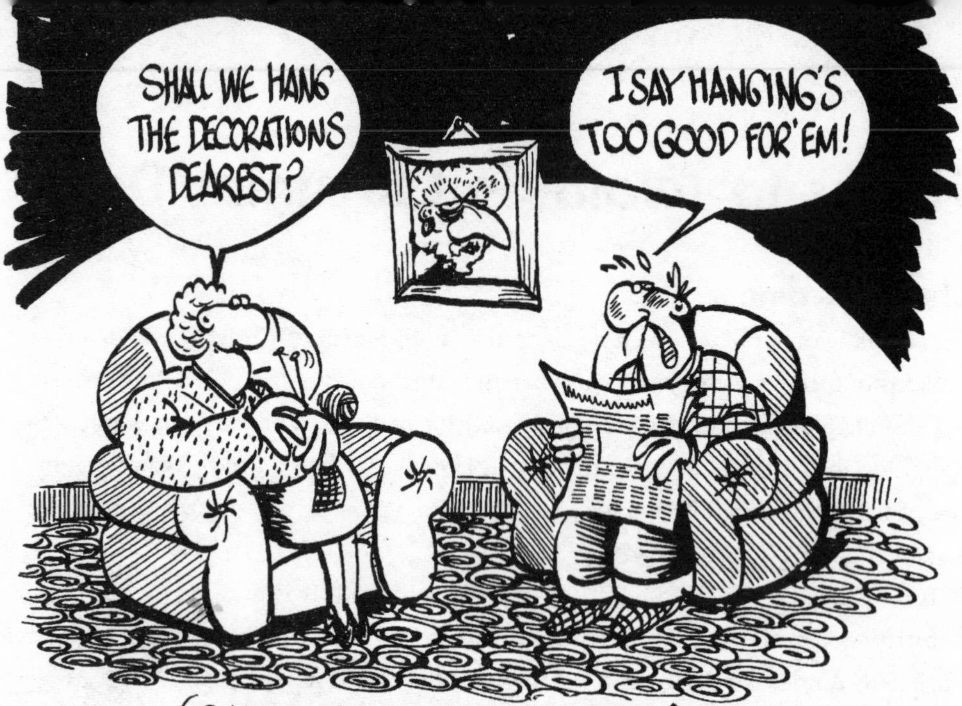
SHALL WE HANG THE DECORATIONS DEAREST?
I SAY HANGING'S TOO GOOD FOR 'EM!
(CHRISTMAS WITH THE TORIES.)

The Americans don't actually celebrate Christmas. They celebrate 'the holiday season' and 'Happy holiday' is a customary greeting the the USA (as is, 'Give us all your money, pal') but, thankfully, this has not yet caught on here, although 'Season's greetings' is becoming more common (as is, 'Give us all your money, pal').

Christmas pudding

Why do we eat this concoction once a year? There is no known answer to this question but we do know that the amount of alcohol in which the pudding is soaked is increasing exponentially each year. This obviously helps to kill the taste while livening up some of the after dinner chat. It also helps to take your mind off the taste and consistency of Christmas pudding to play a game in which each player takes a bite and tries to guess the percentage alcohol in the pudding. Hence the phrase, 'the proof of the pudding is in the eating'.

After dinner games

When the table has been cleared (you can usually get out of this by vomiting up your pudding) it's time for fun and games.

Christmas charades

Like the normal version, except the only title allowed is 'White Christmas'. The fun starts when the family tries to guess whether it's the film or the song that's on your mind. It's a rather short game usually, but gets everyone in the mood and even the really old and infirm can join in without embarrassing themselves too much.

LOOK EVERYBODY, I PICKED UP ENOUGH TURKEY IN THE SALES TO LAST FOR WEEKS !!!

Christmas musical chairs

The only music played is, of course, Bing Crosby's 'White Christmas' and, in the true spirit of Christmas, when the music stops, a chair is added rather than removed. NB: This game can last several days.

Christmas Cluedo

Just like the original board game, except that Santa did it, in the bedroom, with a reindeer antler.

Christmas Monopoly

Simply move around the board, stopping to buy up all the contents of various stores in a frenzy of Christmas shopping. The winner is the player who accumulates the most goods without being sent directly to mass (just like in real life). Community Chest cards offer the chance of a free spiritual Christmas without any fuss and bother.

Christmas poker

The object is to win as much money as possible so that you can start paying your credit card bill.

Christmas Scrabble

In this North Pole version of the famous word game only Eskimo words that mean 'snow' can be used.

And when the games are over there is finally some time to savour the real meaning of Christmas: *Only Fools and Horses*.

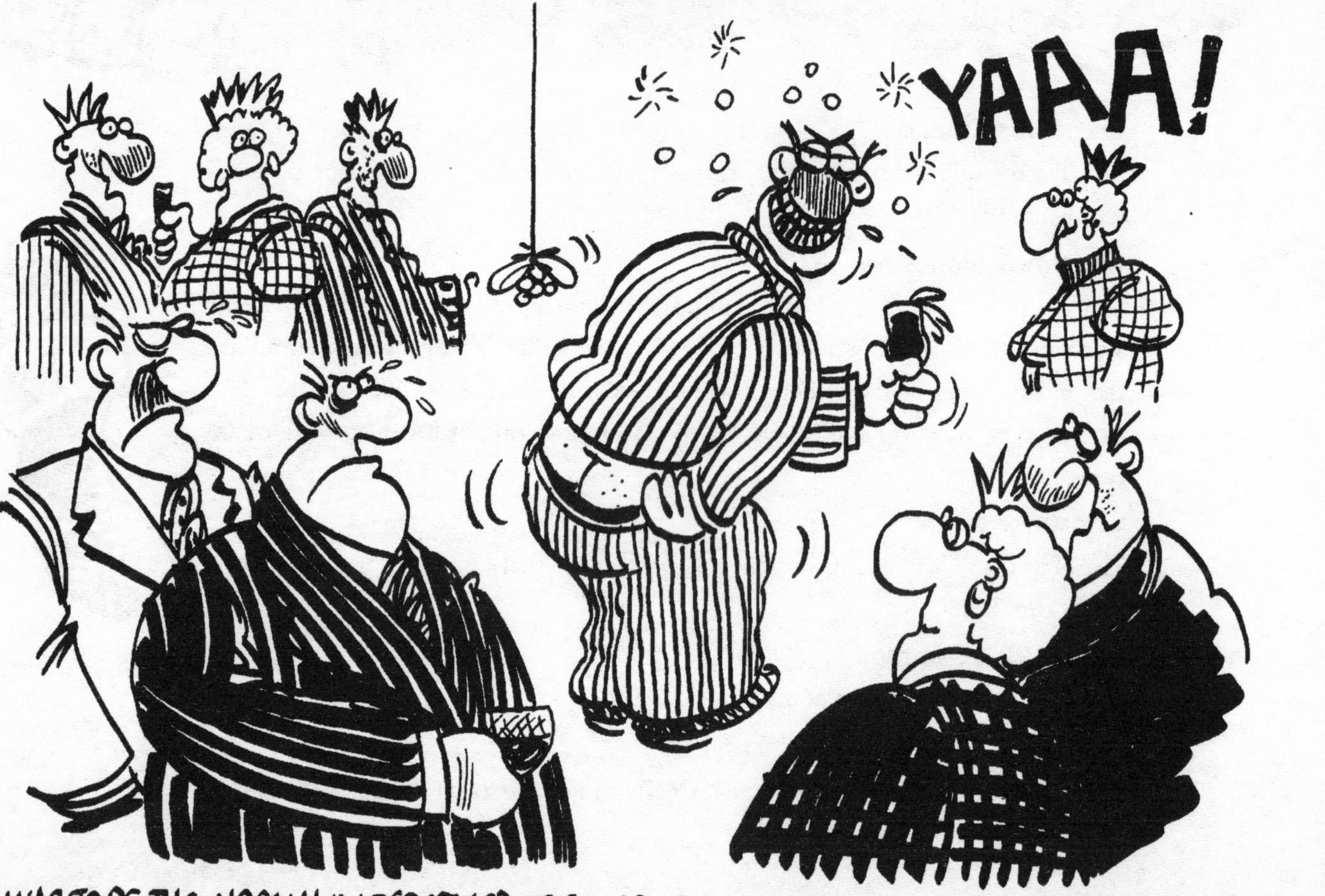
YAAA!

IT WAS TO BE THE NORMALLY RESERVED FOSKINS FROM ACCOUNTS LAST PARTY WITH THE FIRM.

The Christmas Party

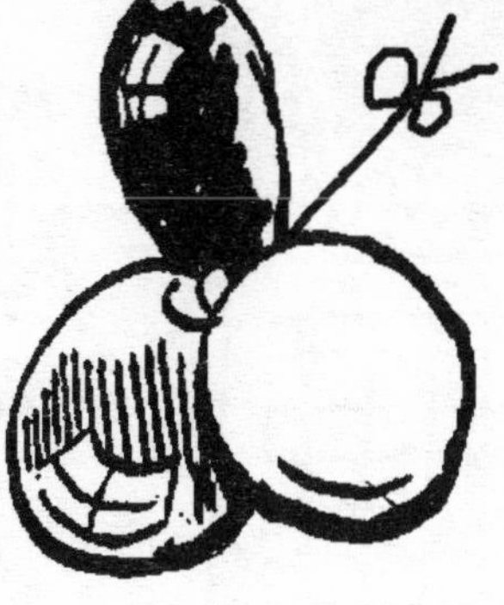

More than anything, Christmas is the party season when everybody takes the opportunity to get ferociously drunk – commonly known as 'entering into the Christmas spirit'. This can be a dangerous time and serious blunders can be made.

What not to wear

False breasts or a funny hat may seem like a good idea at partytime but why not just try wearing simple cotton fabrics, keeping primary colours to a minimum? Remember that you will be forced to wear a colourful paper hat immediately on arrival and this alone will create the demeanour of the party animal. Very high-heeled shoes are a mistake, as they make dancing quite hazardous. This also applies to women. Don't be tempted to wear a colourful bow tie to give the impression that you are 'completely mad'. Rather, attach red crepe paper to your jacket with safety pins or Velcro, which is cheaper but achieves the same desired effect.

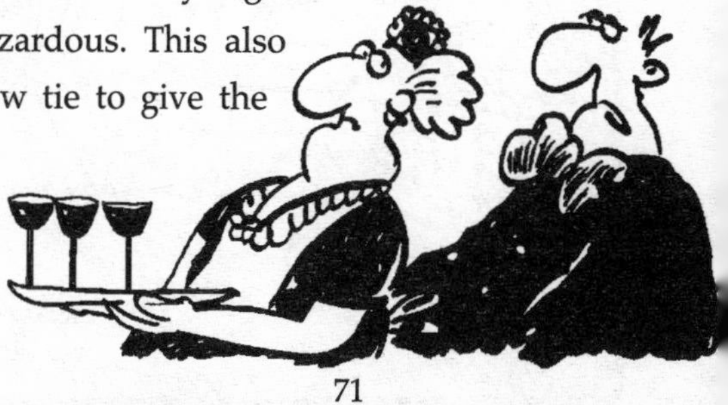

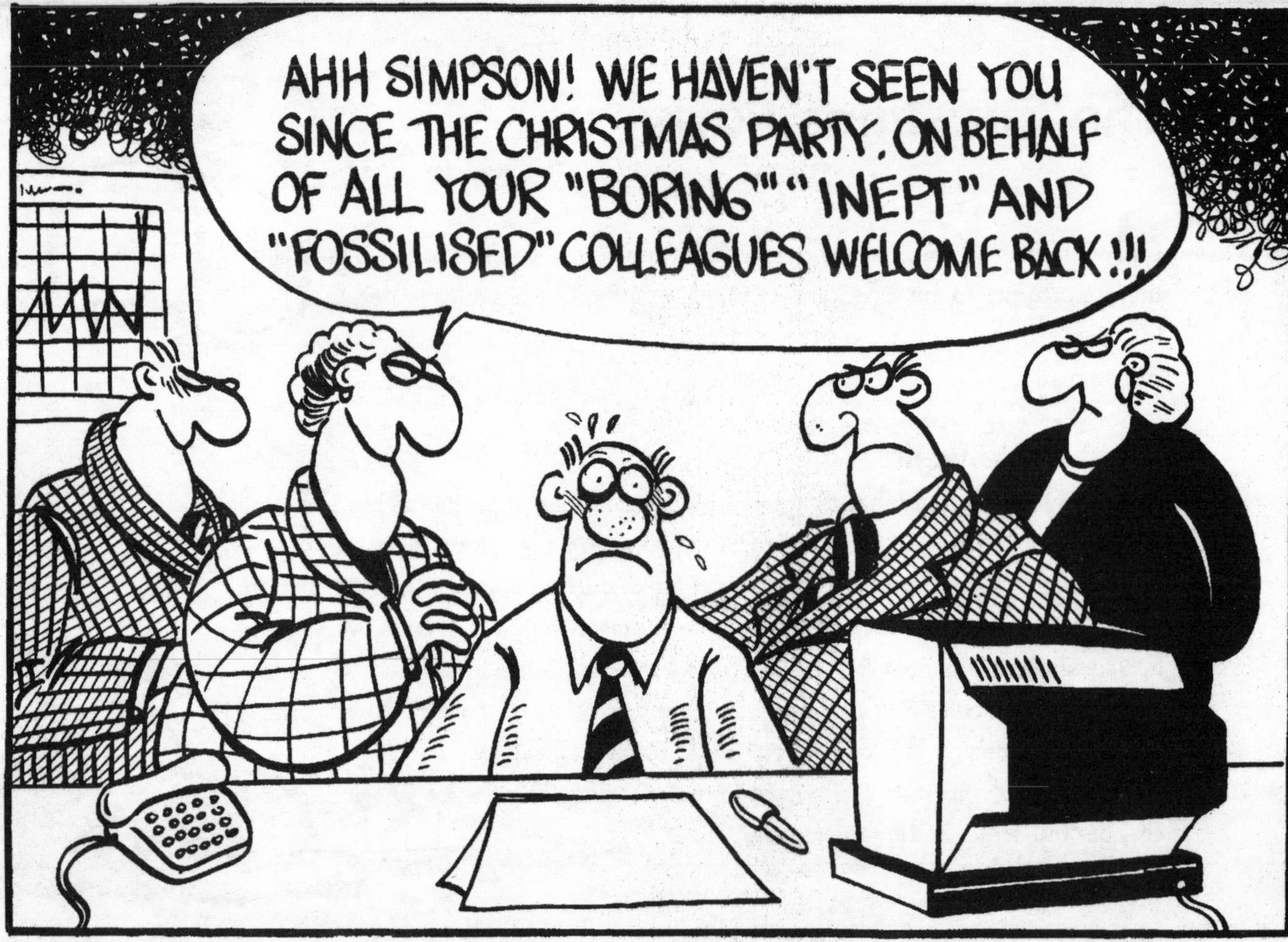
AHH SIMPSON! WE HAVEN'T SEEN YOU SINCE THE CHRISTMAS PARTY. ON BEHALF OF ALL YOUR "BORING" "INEPT" AND "FOSSILISED" COLLEAGUES WELCOME BACK !!!

Ten things people never say at Christmas parties

1 Christmas is for the adults, really.

2 It's so easy to get a taxi at this time of year.

3 Christmas seems to start later every year.

4 Christmas has got so religious.

5 Christmas is simply not a time for the family.

6 Isn't wrapping paper terribly good value?

7 There's some great movies on the telly which I've never seen before.

8 I prefer the shedding variety.

9 You can never have too much mulled wine.

10 A puppy is just for Christmas.

Who to avoid at Christmas parties

- Anybody with a T-shirt that says, 'I'm going to pull a cracker'.
- Anybody who says, 'I'm going to pull a cracker'.
- Anybody who says, 'Hey, let's do the hokey-cokey'.
- Anybody who says, 'What a great idea!'
- Anybody who is crying.
- Anybody who is dying.

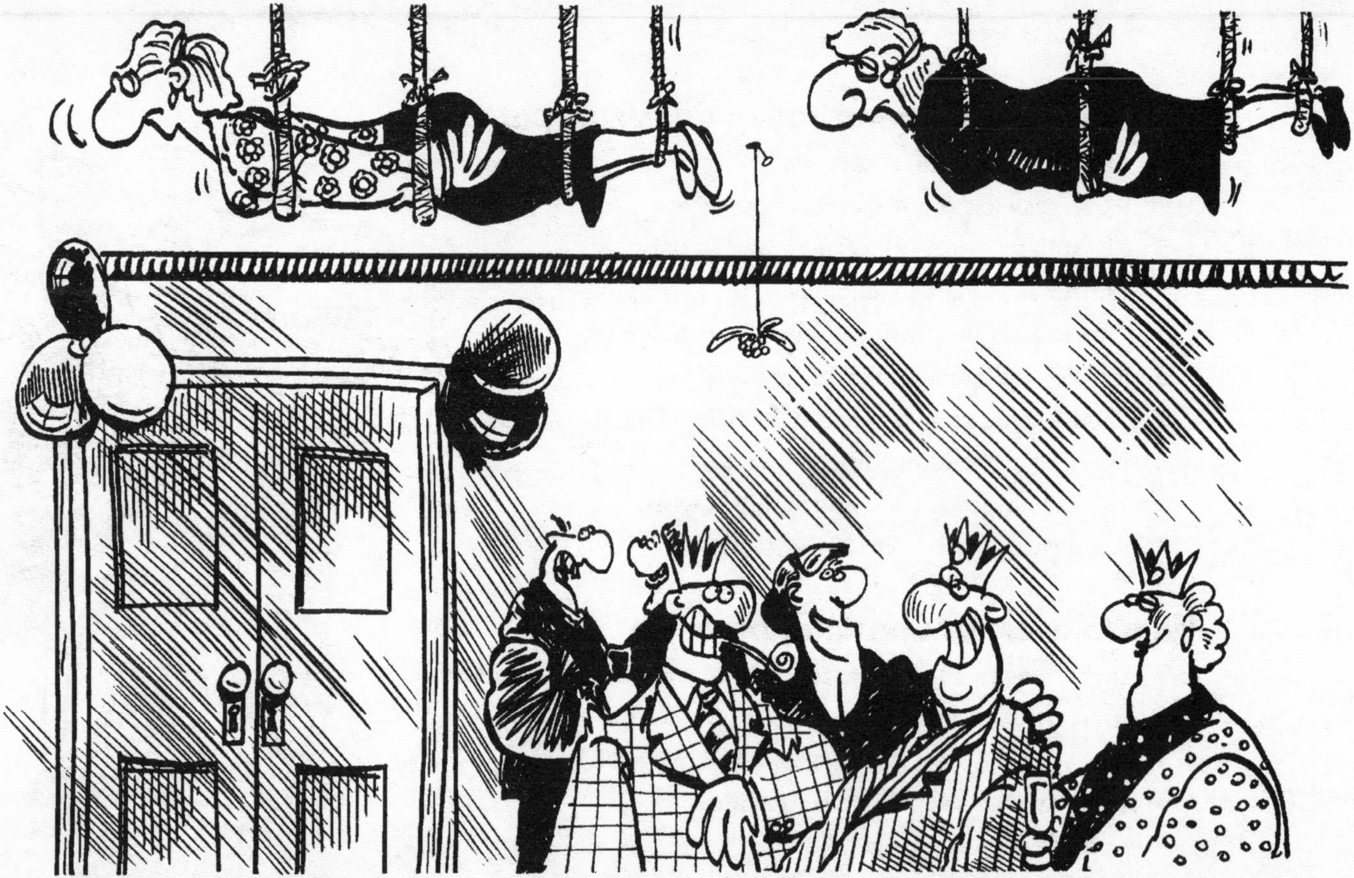

FOR THE UNFORTUNATELY NAMED HOLLY AND IVY EMPLOYEES AT HODGKINS AND CO CHRISTMAS HAD BECOME SOMETHING OF A NIGHTMARE...

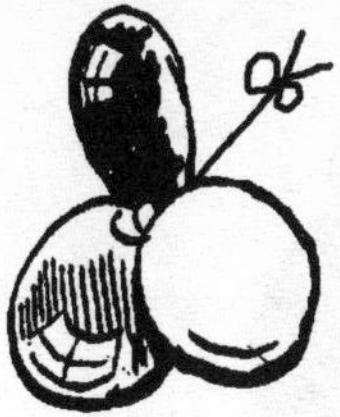

- Anybody who dresses as Santa Claus throughout the year.
- Anybody who says that they've seen the real Santa Claus.
- Anybody who says they are the real Santa Claus.
- Anybody with a 'crazy' waistcoat.
- Anybody who wears paper hats all year round.
- Anybody who drinks mulled wine all year round.
- Anybody who says, 'Christmas in prison isn't half as much fun'.
- Anybody who refers to 'Christmas on my planet'.

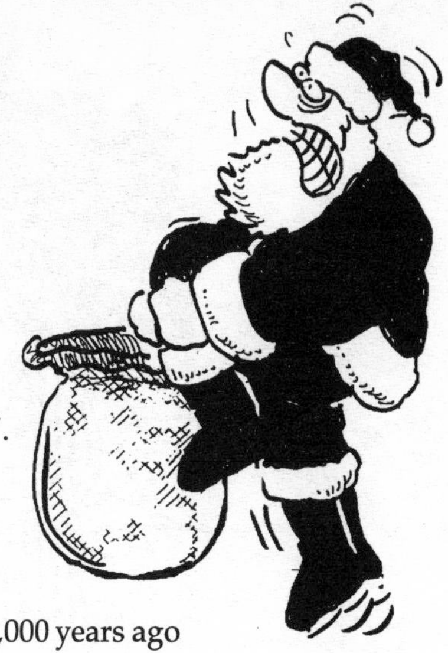

The office party

The very first Christmas office party took place in Bethlehem almost 2,000 years ago when the shepherds who attended the birth of Jesus decided to make the most of the night and wet the baby's head. They awoke late the following morning with only a vague recollection of what had passed and all of their sheep had been savaged by wolves. As a result, they had to become beggars to survive. Nevertheless, the tradition of the Christmas office party soon caught on, albeit with profound consequences, most notably for the ancient Romans. The decline and fall of their empire has been directly attributed to one particularly wild Christmas party.

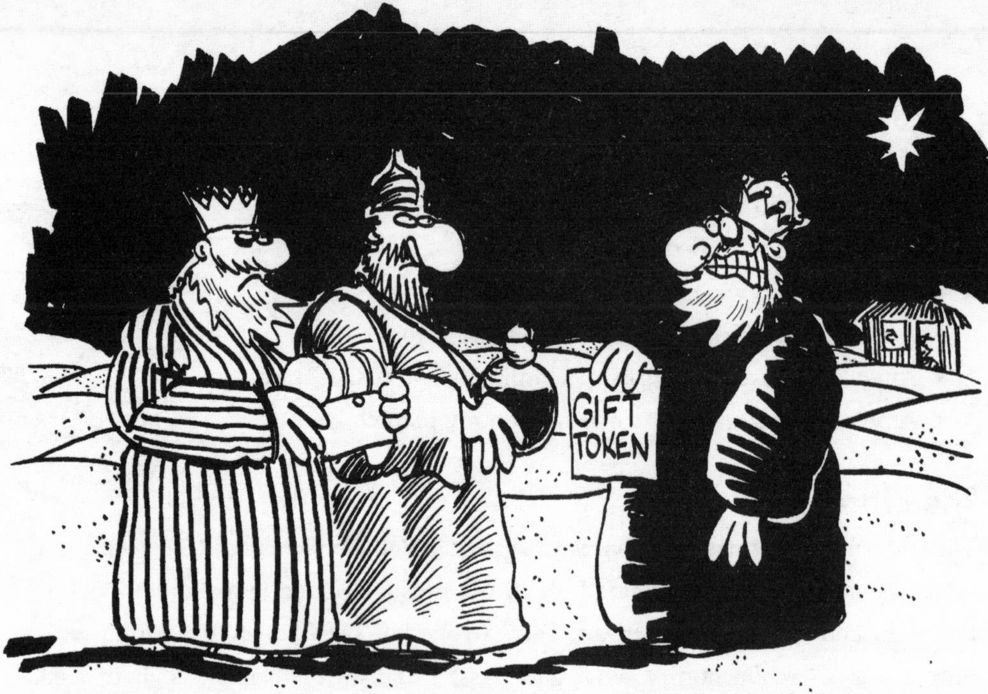
GIFT
TOKEN

To this day, all over the world people wake up the morning after the Christmas office party wishing they had not attended it. Over the years, this tradition has become a sordid affair, characterised by excessive alcohol consumption and physical contact between staff members. To avoid the worst pitfalls, certain precautions should be taken.

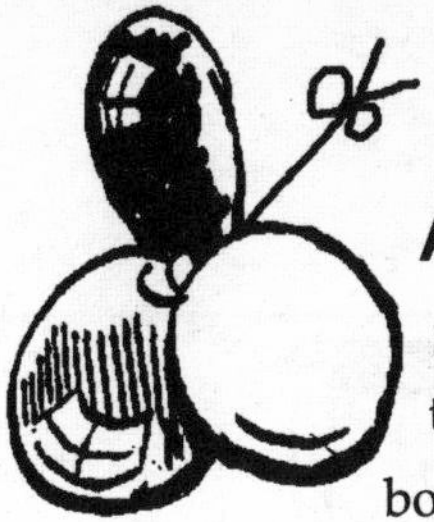

A Do not strip down to your socks and shoes late in the night. This is never a good idea, no matter how appealing it appears at the time. It is absolutely certain that the next day you will find it difficult to discuss strategic matters with the boss.

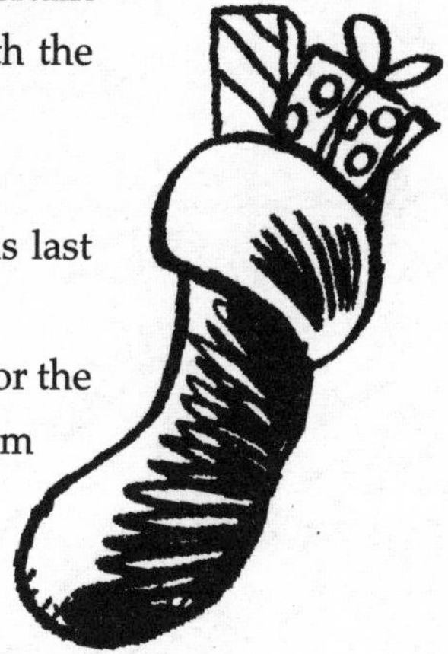

B Never kiss your superior or challenge him/her to an arm wrestle (see A).

C Never say: 'I think I might go try the Sambuca now . . .' These are famous last words and can lead to both A and B above as well as D.

D Never ignite your own anal gaseous emissions, as this is rarely applauded for the physical feat of daring that it is and has been known to hamper long-term promotion prospects.

E Do not photocopy any part of your anatomy. This is both dangerous and considered symptomatic of numerous character defects.

F Never assume that the Christmas office party is a chance to 'let your hair down' and an opportunity for 'the workers and management to treat each other as equals'. Bosses never treat staff as equals, even if they find themselves wearing party hats and pulling crackers. Any assumption to the contrary can lead to unwise talk along the following lines: 'Can I be brutally frank, sir? . . . ' Compared to this faux pas, stripping stark naked and dancing on the tables while singing 'Jingle Bells' shows true management potential.

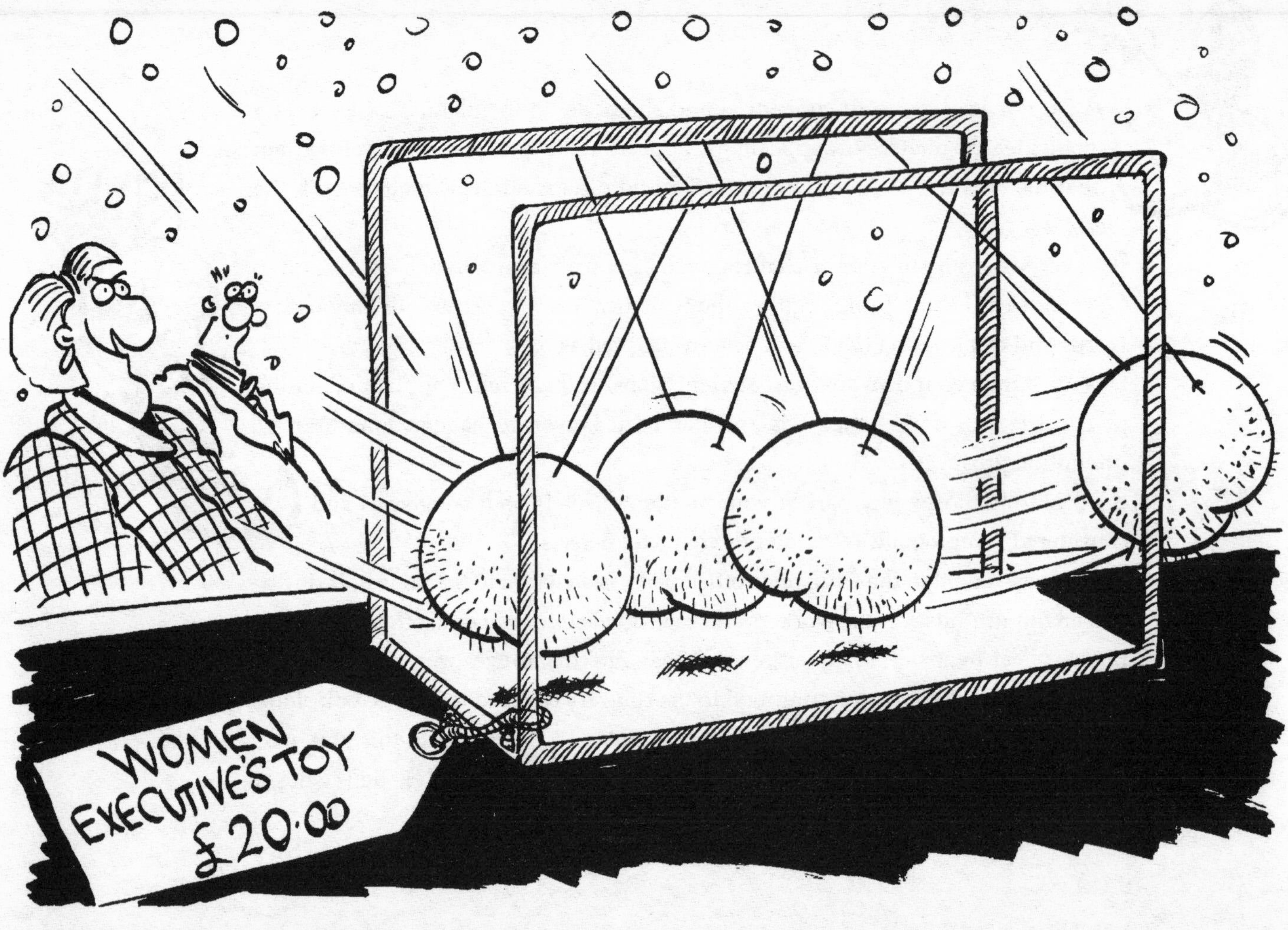
WOMEN EXECUTIVE'S TOY
£20.00

We Wish You a Politically Correct Christmas

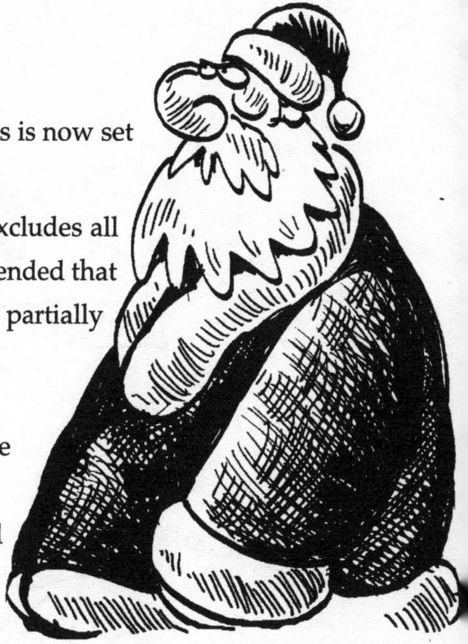

Christmas is one of the last bastions of the politically incorrect but this is now set to change.

Santa Claus White male father figure. This description immediately excludes all women, as well as persons of African and Asian descent. It is recommended that this old-fashioned character be replaced with a vertically challenged, partially sighted, female African.

Mistletoe To be replaced with Mistertoe on occasion.

Xmas There is no good reason why the letter X should be chosen above all others in the alphabet. In future, the letter preceding 'mas' will rotate on an annual basis with Y to fill the next slot, then 'Zmas', and so on.

Christmas In this day and age it appears inappropriate to name the Yuletide festival after a dead white Jewish male. This problem could be solved by using more culturally diverse figures. For example, we could

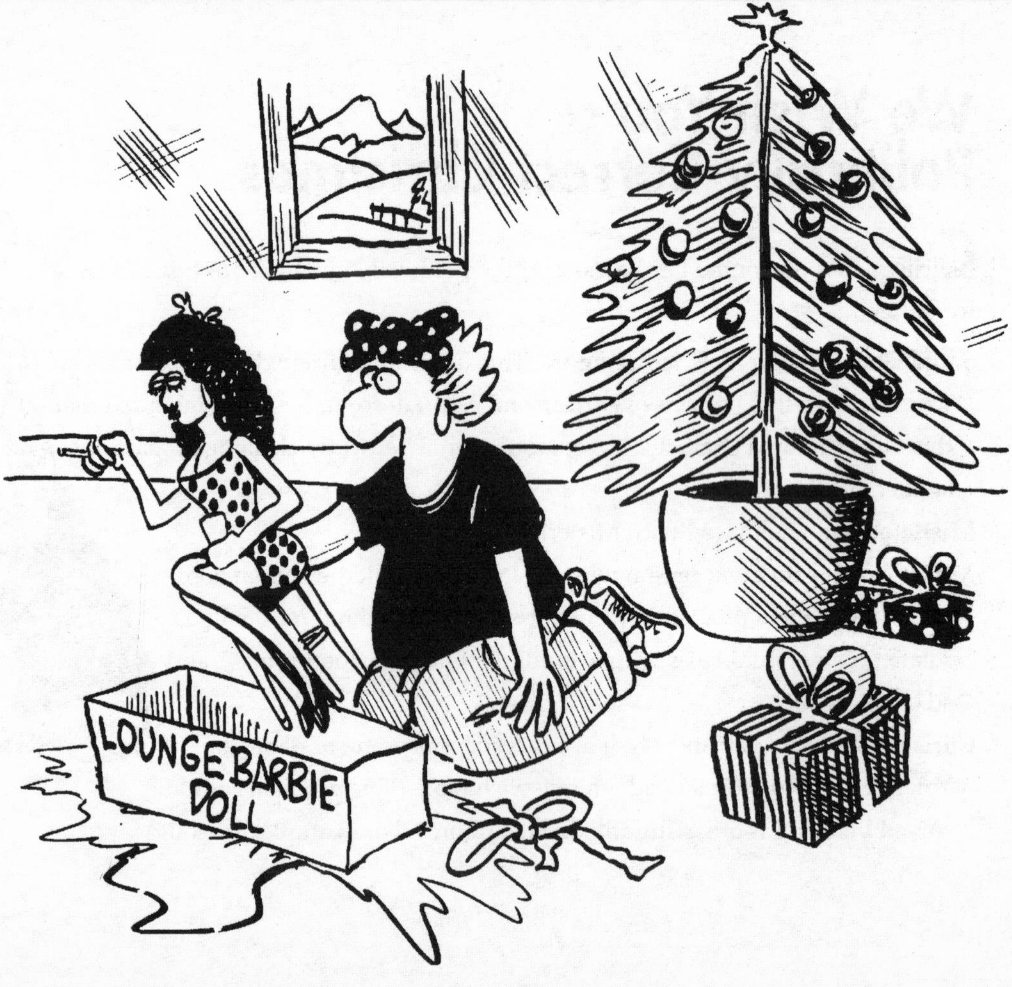
LOUNGE BARBIE
DOLL

celebrate Joan of Arcmas, Gandhimas, Genghis Khanmas, etc.

Tree The Christmas tree has long been part of the Yuletide tradition but the time has come to open up the position to other forms of botanical life. A Christmas bush or Christmas moss would provide decoration and endless variety, while reducing the problem of shedding.

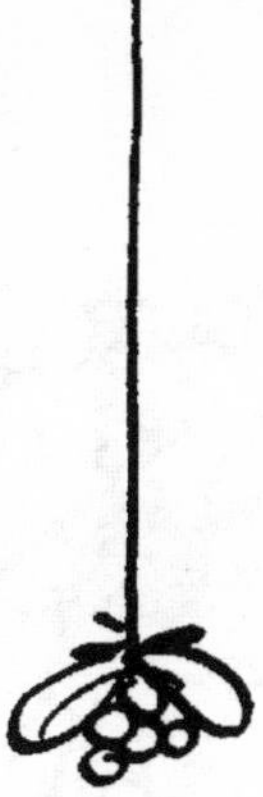

Reindeer As with the Christmas tree, the pulling of Santa's sleigh has been controlled by one species for too long. At present it is difficult to recommend another mammal with the same pull-to-weight ratio, which is also capable of flight, although advances in genetic engineering could yet overcome this problem.

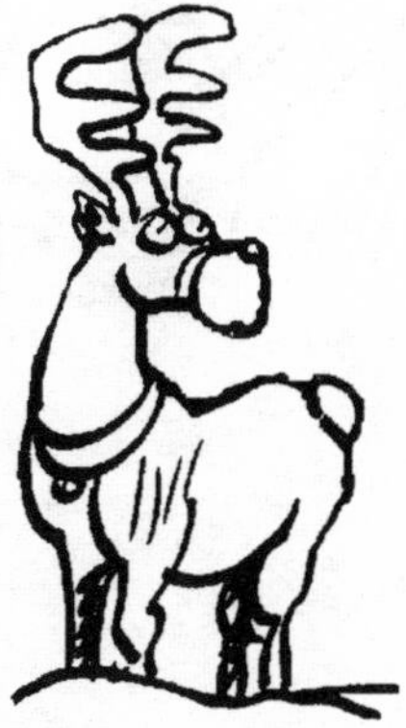

Holly and Ivy Both these names are overly gender specific. Their replacement with Derek and Mavis would appeal to a broader cross-section of the community.

Hymns To be substituted with 'hers' on appropriate occasions, but generally by 'its'.

Carol The introduction of a male Christian name for certain popular Christmas tunes would go a long way to introducing a note of harmony here. For example, 'Away in a Manger' would be a 'carol' while 'Good King Wenceslas' would be a 'clive'.

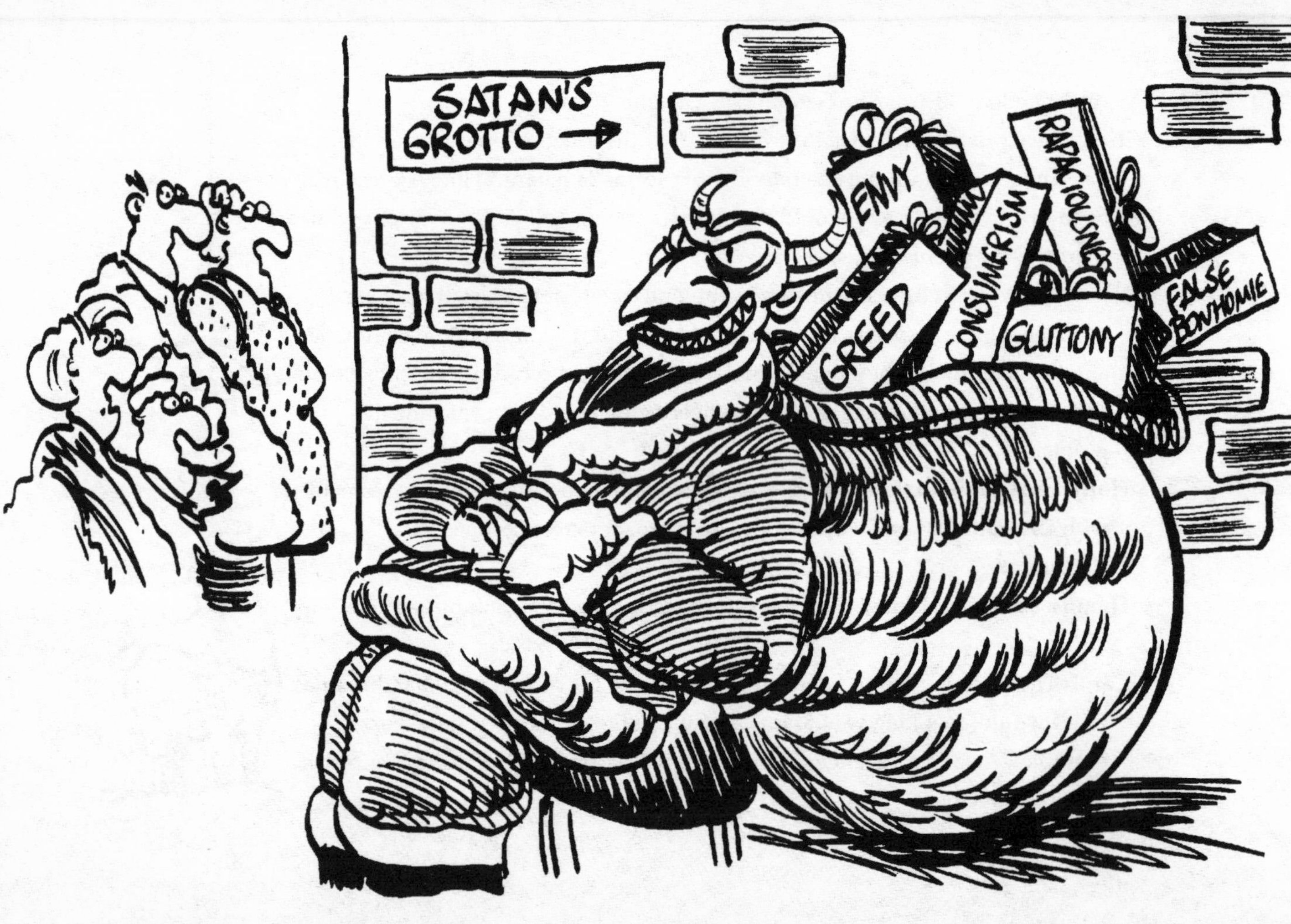
SATAN'S GROTTO →
ENVY
GREED
CONSUMERISM
RAPACIOUSNESS
GLUTTONY
FALSE BONHOMIE

Fairy lights This homophobic term for Christmas tree illumination is antiquated and offensive and will be replaced initially with 'person lights'. There is still some debate about the word 'light', excluding as it does the more physically overdeveloped members of our society and, eventually, the term 'person mediums' will be phased in.

Action Man Still popular at Christmas, this toy will be renamed 'Play Person' to remove the obvious references to violence and gender stereotyping.

Snow An essential part of the Christmas image, the predominance of the colour white in snow renders it offensive to many cultures. In future snow will be replaced with the colour-neutral rain and popular Christmas songs such as 'White Christmas' will be renamed accordingly – for example, 'Glassy Christmas'.

Cracker The phrase 'to pull a cracker' carries with it overtones of sexual conquest and loutish behaviour. In future the phrase will be 'to share a tug'.

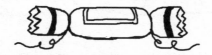

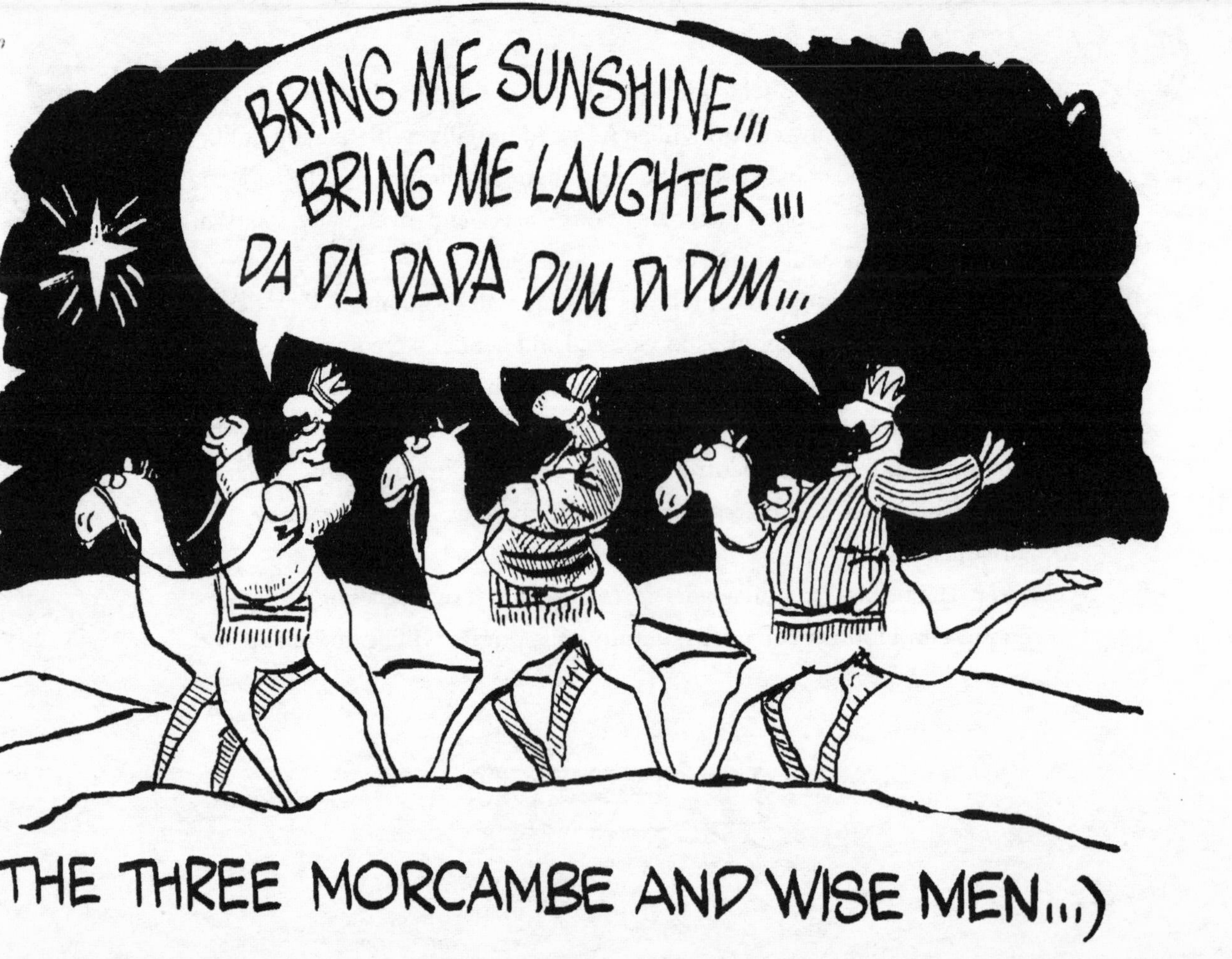
BRING ME SUNSHINE...
BRING ME LAUGHTER...
DA DA DADA DUM DI DUM...

(...THE THREE MORCAMBE AND WISE MEN...)

Tarantino's Nativity

FADE IN:

Thumping soundtrack as camera swoops in on two local shepherds, FRANKIE and JOHNNY, in a field outside Bethlehem. They appear to be talking to an angel who tells them to go to a stable where the son of God is to be born.

FRANKIE and JOHNNY Wow.

CUT TO:

The road to Bethlehem from Nazareth

MARY Jeez, Joey, are we nearly there yet? I'm ready to pop.

JOEY Listen, babe, we'll stop at Bethlehem and get a room at the Holiday Inn. Now, quit complaining.

MARY But I'm pregnant, Joey.

JOEY Hey, that's got nothing to do with me, remember? I never even laid a hand on ya.

CUT TO:

Somewhere far away a group of wise guys are arguing

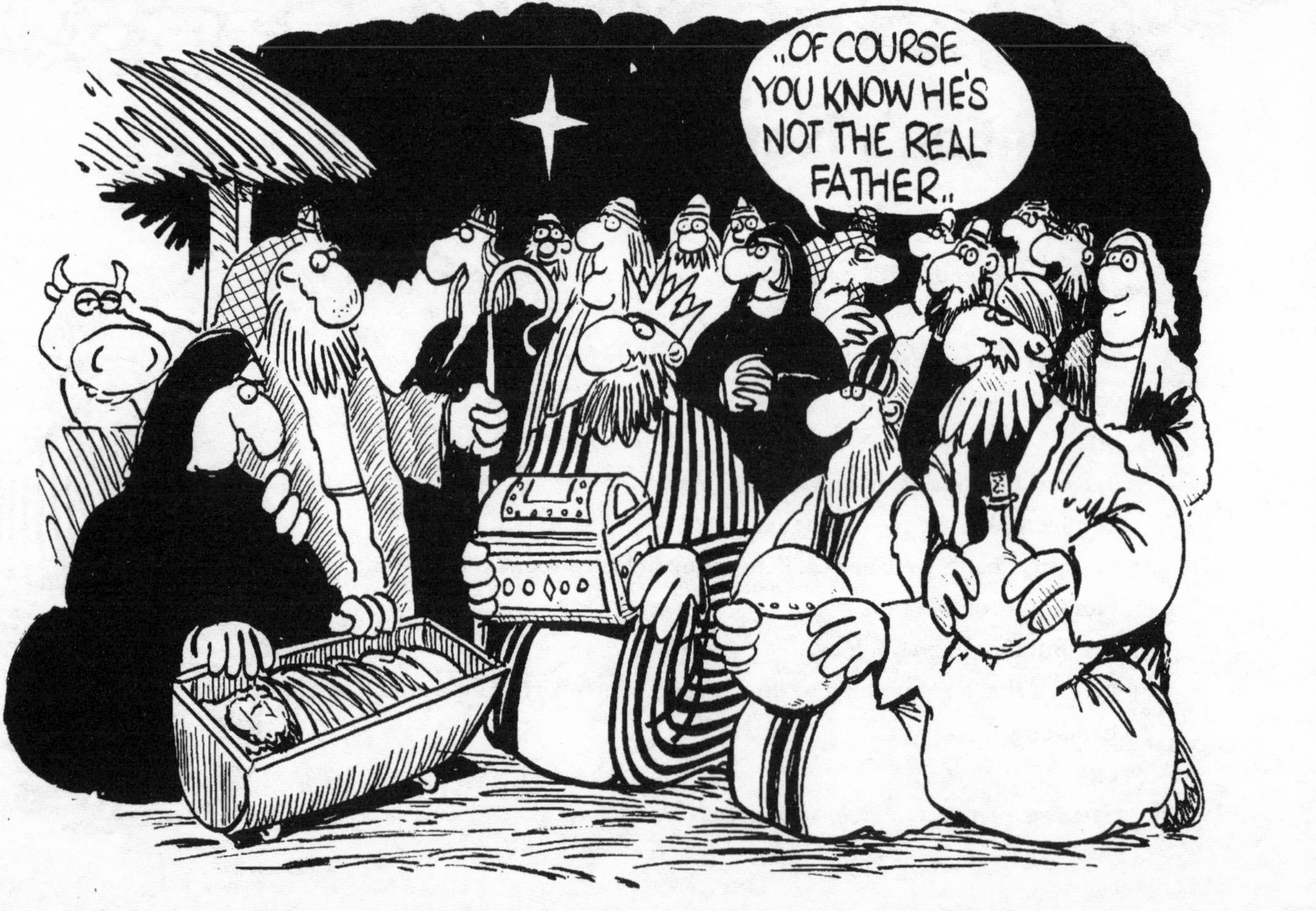
..OF COURSE YOU KNOW HE'S NOT THE REAL FATHER..

CAS Yoh, Balt, let's sample this merchandise.

BALT Listen, Cas, the goods stay in the briefcases until we deliver.

MEL But this is real good stuff, completely pure – we gotta sample it.

BALT Mel, you motherf**ker, I know the frankincense and myrrh are completely uncut but that's the way it stays. And keep your paws off the gold, do you hear me?

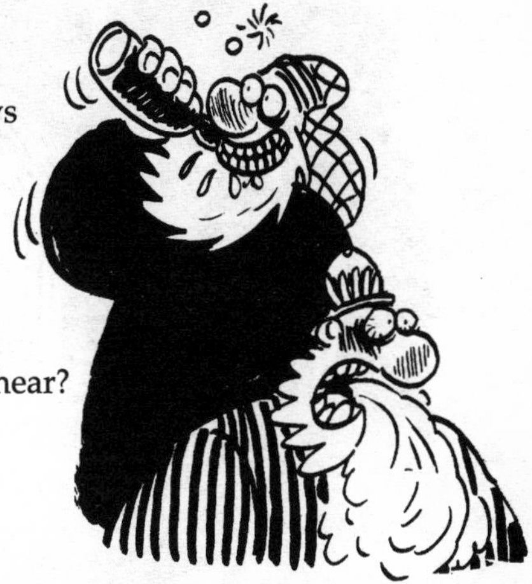

CUT TO:

Somewhere in Galilee

HEROD'S HONEY You're one mean dude, Herod. A real bad cat!

HEROD You better believe it, man. I'm the main man, the King, do ya hear? I'm the King. Baby, let me be, your lovin' teddy bear . . .

HONEY Sure thing, boss, you're the King.

CUT TO:

Bethlehem

INNKEEPER Nah, there's no room at the Holiday Inn, man – it's the Christmas bank holiday weekend.

JOEY What d'ya mean?

INNKEEPER Are you deaf or something? I said there's no f**king room at the f**king inn.

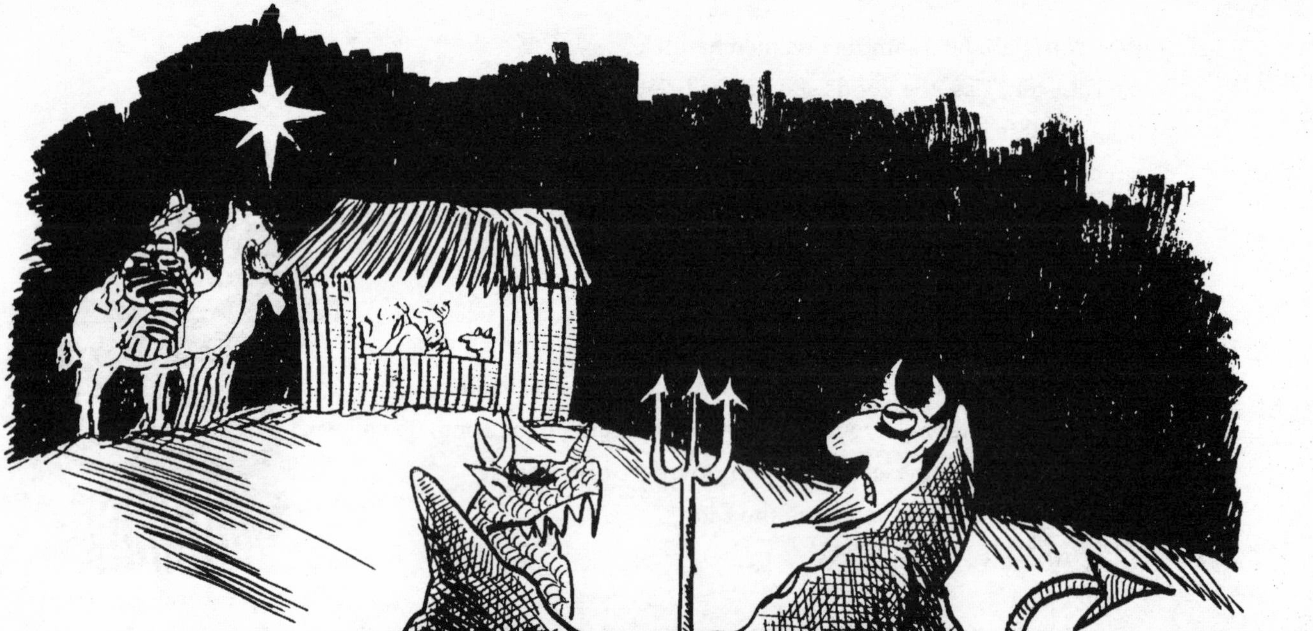

"CHEER UP BOSS... WITHIN TWO THOUSAND YEARS ALL THIS WILL BE A SORDID SHAM GLORIFYING CRASS COMMERCIALISM."

JOEY Hey, watch your goddamn language in front of the lady.

MARY Joey, I need to find a place real bad.

JOEY Would I let you down, babe? You'll get premier treatment, I swear.

CUT TO:

Back with the shepherds, FRANKIE *and* JOHNNY *decide the vision was for real and the drugs are not responsible.*

FRANKIE Let's split for the stable, man.

JOHNNY What about the sheep?

FRANKIE Sheep! Sheep! We're talking Lamb of God here.

JOHNNIE Wow.

CUT TO:

Bethlehem

JOEY What about this place, babe?

MARY It's a goddamn stable, Joey. Are you *crazy?*

JOEY Just get inside, babe.

MARY But I want an epidural.

JOEY I told you, there's no more drugs. We're clean, remember?

CUT TO:

Inside the stable

MARY Drugs, I need some drugs.

JOEY Listen, babe, natural childbirth is where it's at these days –

MARY Just get me some f**king pain relief – frankincense, myrrh, anything at all.

Enter the three wise guys

BALT Yoh – we've got some quality merchandise here for the lady.

MARY Thank God – let me have it.

Enter the shepherds, to the surprise of the Magi

CAS Who the f**k are you guys?

FRANKIE The angel sent us.

MEL Who the f**k's The Angel – do you guys work for Herod?

JOHNNY Who?

BALT They're after our stuff, man – let's waste them –

The row is interrupted by the cry of a newborn baby – it's a boy!

JOHNNY What a beautiful sound, man.

All look at the new baby, but then BALT makes a move for his sword. The shepherds are quick and their crooks are lethal and a split second later the Magi and shepherds lie slowly bleeding to death. MARY, JOEY and the infant are left with three briefcases of gold, frankincense and myrrh.

MARY It's a goddamn miracle.

JOEY You're right, babe – now we'll live like kings and Joey Jnr will never want for anything.

MARY Er, about that name, Joey . . .

THE END

FADES OUT TO:

Guitar music and the Elvis version of 'Glory, Glory'